Sōshitsu Sen XVI

Urasenke Tea Procedure Guidebook 1
Introductory Level
Fundamental Techniques
Bonryaku Temae
Chitose-bon Temae
Knowledge for Guests

TANKOSHA

兜門

Kabutomon

The Kabutomon, "Helmet Gate," may be said to be the symbol of the Urasenke historical estate in Kyoto, Urasenke Konnichian. The bark-shingle roof and rain troughs of bamboo make for an unpretentious, tastefully wabi appearance. Beyond this gate lies the Urasenke tea room complex, a place with a long, rich history and time-honored heritage.

Technical Remarks

The romanization of Japanese is according to the Hepburn system. Long vowels in the Japanese words are indicated by a macron (¯), except in cases of words already known by an alternate spelling (e.g., noh) and place names which are widely known (e.g., Kyoto). Hyphenation is used sparingly to indicate the word elements in Japanese compound terms.

This English-language guidebook necessarily includes a large number of Japanese terms, for there are so many terms used in chadō which do not have English counterparts; among them, some of the most basic and common terms. Concerning the italicization of Japanese terms in this book, the most basic chadō terms are treated as English loanwords, and therefore are not italicized. In most cases, Japanese terms are defined in parentheses on first appearance. Also, a glossary of most of the terms is provided at the back.

Throughout this book, names of people are given in the order that is customary in the person's native country. The exception is the author's name on the title page, on the jacket and spine, and in the copyright information. Here the names are given in accordance with the international standards used in libraries and bookstores.

Urasenke Tea Procedure Guidebook 1
Introductory Level

This book is a translation of the Japanese guidebook *Urasenke Chadō Temae Kyōsoku 1* authored by Sōshitsu Sen XVI and published by Tankosha Publishing Co., Ltd. on October 16, 2010.

Published on April 11, 2017, by Tankosha Publishing Co., Ltd., Kyoto.

© 2017 by Sōshitsu Sen, Chairman, Urasenke Foundation
All rights reserved

English translation
　Urasenke Tankokai Federation International Affairs Department
　(Gretchen Mittwer and Michael Hardy)

Photographs
　Masaki Miyano, Minao Tabata, Toshitaka Ogasawara

Design
　Sein Inc., Kyoto

Printing and binding
　Dai Nippon Printing Co., Ltd.

Printed in Japan
ISBN978-4-473-04178-4

Introduction   4

For Those Beginning the Study of Chadō   7

The Urasenke Family Lineage   13

Before Beginning to Take Lessons   22

Fundamental Techniques   25

Mannerly Deportment   26
- Standing and Walking   26
- Sitting and Standing Up   27
- Bowing – the Three Types of Bows   28
- Opening and Closing Fusuma Sliding Doors   30

Temae Fundamentals   32
- Handling the Fukusa   32
- Examining the Chasen, Folding the Chakin, and Wiping the Chawan   46
- Handling the Hishaku   52
- Preparations in the Mizuya   60

Bonryaku Temae   61

Chitose-bon Temae   87

Knowledge for Guests   117

Entering the Tea Room   118
- The Tsukubai   118
- Tea Room Types   121
- Entering Through a Nijiriguchi   122
- Entering a Small Tea Room   125
- Entering a Spacious Tea Room   127

How to Partake of the Confections and Usucha   130
- Partaking of Higashi   131
- Partaking of an Omogashi Which Is Individually Served   134
- Partaking of Omogashi Which Are Served in a Serving Bowl   135
- Partaking of Usucha   136
- Partaking of Usucha When There Are Multiple Guests   139

Glossary   144

Urasenke Tea Procedure Guidebook 1
Table of Contents

Introduction
by Sen Sōshitsu XVI
Grand Master, the Urasenke Chadō Tradition

A fundamental rule at chadō study sessions is that note-taking is not allowed. Most likely every chadō student can recall having completed a practice temae and, returning to the mizuya, hurriedly scribbling down a memo about a point that was corrected by the teacher. Particularly in the case of the sixteen *konarai* tea procedures, such notes often go into quite a bit of detail, it seems. Come to think of it, I still keep a lot of memos that I wrote.

Just because you immediately make a note of a point, however, you should not rest at ease. Likewise, I do not want people to think that they are safe because there are guidebooks. It would truly be a shame if people feel that even without learning the temae through real experience, they are fine because all they have to do is open up the guidebook and it will quickly teach them. I want you to use this book at those times when you practice over and over and yet cannot completely remember everything; as an auxiliary resource when you forget something. As I have constantly maintained, tea-procedure guidebooks are no more than a collection of memoranda to keep by your side as you undergo your training. Unless you make good of your time at your study sessions and see and hear everything you ought to learn, you will hardly gain command of chadō by reading a guidebook about it.

Genpaku Sōtan, the grandson of Sen Rikyū, left these words: "Chanoyu is something imparted to the mind, to the eyes, to the ears; not through even a single stroke of writing." Indeed, in chadō, innumerable thoughts and sentiments have been conveyed from mind to mind, person to person, for over four hundred years within the flow leading from teacher to disciple and from that disciple to the next. As such, the one-and-only way to study chadō is to squarely approach the question of why you are preparing the bowl of tea in the first place, uncovering the answer through earnest physical practice, and etching that into your heart. I will be happy if you use this Urasenke tea procedure guidebook to assist you in this path of study.

中門

Chūmon

The *chūmon*, "middle gate," in the *roji* (garden approach to the tea rooms) at Urasenke Konnichian. It separates the outer and inner sections of the roji, the *sotoroji* and *uchiroji*. Passing through this middle gate and following the stepping stones leading through the inner roji, one reaches Urasenke's representative tea rooms, the Konnichian and the Yūin.

For Those Beginning the Study of Chadō

A Practice Session Is Tantamount to an Actual Tea Gathering

Mastering the Basics

The verses known as the *Rikyū Hyakushu* (Rikyū's Hundred Verses) express the spirit of Sen Rikyū's chadō in verse form, and among them is this: "Practice constitutes learning from one, becoming cognizant of ten, then returning from ten to one, the beginning." This tells us that, within this path of study, it is important to learn the basics through repeated practice, and finally at the stage when those basics have been mastered, it is a reasonable matter of course that, from there, you can enjoy chanoyu done with expedience; chanoyu which is relaxing.

At Urasenke headquarters, Kyoto, there are intensive seminars held in winter and summer, and study seminars held in spring and fall. Each one of them begins with review of the basics. This is because a person may have practiced the basic *usucha*, *koicha*, *shozumi*, and *gozumi* procedures many times, and may think he is accustomed to them, but his movements actually may not be satisfactory.

I often do service at temples and shrines by conducting ritual tea offerings (*kenchashiki*), and the temae does not always turn out the way my mental image had pictured it beforehand. Depending upon the slightest difference in the conditions, I can sense a difference when I sit before the daisu. Of course it is very subtle, and because of it the temae does not fall apart or anything. I am made to realize, however, just how important it is to finely tune the balance between mind and body when preparing to do temae, and how difficult that can be.

It is only when a person, in learning to carry out a temae, has become capable of spontaneously dealing with out-of-the-ordinary inner senses and outer conditions, that he can say that he has a command of the temae. In order to achieve this goal, one must continue to review the basics. In other words, there is no end to the study of the basics.

Your Posture

In the Way of Tea, it is desirable to be natural and relaxed, mentally and physically; that is, it is desirable to have a natural appearance. Begin with trying to sit seiza as you would naturally. You should not appear to be forcing yourself to sit rigidly, nor should you appear slack. It could be described as 'sitting at ease.' Your right hand is clasping your left hand on your lap, but now rest your hands on your thighs, as when you sit at the temaeza for tea preparation. This is your natural form, your "posture" (*kamae*).

Chadō training begins with *warigeiko*, or "divided practice" of the basic elements, which purpose is for the student to firmly establish his "posture," and is not to force everyone into the same rigid mold. Every person has his own individual posture. The posture which you master through *warigeiko* will become the basis of your demeanor. From your temae to the way you bow and walk, your body will move flexibly and synchronously with your breathing. Please stop and reflect upon your natural carriage, and find a posture of your own, a *kamae*, that will make the most of your natural carriage.

The Preciousness of the Study Sessions (*Keiko*)

The *Kojiki* (Record of Ancient Matters; 712 A.D.) is the oldest chronicle of Japan, and in it we find this statement: *Keiko shōkon*, or "Study of the past illuminates the present." *Keiko* refers to the activity of studying the various things which have continued from antiquity to modern times, and the statement teaches that the present becomes clear to one through this study. Thinking of it this way, your daily chadō study session, whether it is taking place at a study seminar or at your regular place of practice, presents you with a golden opportunity that particular day in your life.

One of the important attitudes you should possess in his approach to the study of chadō is that a study session is tantamount to an actual tea gathering. Though it may be a practice temae, I would like for you to undertake it imagining that you are hosting a tea gathering. Even during your preparations in the mizuya, I want you to carefully consider the ambience that day and select a combination of implements which you have put your heart into, instead of being inclined to choose the combination without giving it much thought.

It may only be in chadō that what happens at a practice session is the same as what happens at a real event, an actual tea gathering: a scroll is hung in the room, flowers are put in, the various implements are made ready, and the guest is served confections and tea. It would be such a waste to think of this propitious, precious time as simply "practice." Even at your regular place of practice, I hope that you will always approach your study sessions with the attitude that you are the host or the guest at a tea gathering, a real chadō function.

The Temae of the Urasenke Chadō Tradition

In the Urasenke chadō tradition, it was in the era of the 11th-generation iemoto, Gengensai (1810–77), that the gate to the study of temae was opened so that men and women alike could learn chadō. Gengensai, known as the originator of the *chabakodate* tea-making procedures, the *ryūrei* style, and the *dairo* tea-making procedures, also contributed to the tradition by standardizing the placement of the right hand over the left when sitting as a guest, the use of the foot closer to the guests when entering a room, and so on.

In the Konnichian Library, there is an extant record of the lessons taught by Gengensai as he traveled around Japan. It is entitled *Kissasōgeiki* [Record of Tea-drinking Send-offs and Welcomes], and was written by Watanabe Yūjitsuan, Gengensai's elder brother. In the preface, Gengensai says that confusion is easily caused because the style of chanoyu practiced by the various families differs. Therefore, students of the Urasenke chadō tradition should use this *Kissasōgeiki* as the first step in their studies, he says. This same record also states, "Though we say 'throughout the Sen Family generations,' each generation has done some adopting and rejecting in their time." This gives us an insight into the impetus that led Gengensai to revise the tea-making procedures.

Twelve years after the completion of the *Kissasōgeiki*, Gengensai released another book, the *Kissakōmongashi* [Tile Shard for Knocking on the Tea-drinking Gate], in which the following is written: "A temae should be quite free of glossiness, and for this, it should be something without highlights and one needs to turn resolutely away from giving in to the temptation of showing off in front of others or trying to appear skillful." He reiterates his previous caution against conducting temae as though conducting a performance, and newly mentions that temae which have shed their glossiness are good.

The term "*gyōtei*" used in reference to the Urasenke Konnichian deputy tea masters derives from a phrase in the *Kissakōmongashi* which states, "It is most important to make a delicious bowl of tea. If one's actions (*gyō*) and mind are not in accord, the tea will not be well-made, but when they are as one body (*tei*), the tea is made extremely well." Thus, the term "*gyōtei*" indicates that a person of this position's actions and mind are in accord, and it is with this meaning that the term has been in use at Urasenke since the time of Gengensai.

Passing Forward the Teachings

Something that I say quite often is that it is fine for there to be various ways of enjoying chanoyu, but the principles must never be forgotten. When I say "the principles," I mean the essential spirit of "*Wa Kei Sei Jaku*," or "Harmony, Respect, Purity, Tranquility," which Sen Rikyū identified. We must take to heart this canon which Rikyū left for us and apply it in whatever situation we face.

I will not go into detail here about the meaning of the four terms, but if your first thought upon reading the canon is that it seems knotty, it would mean that you are only seeing one aspect of it.

"Harmony, Respect, Purity, Tranquility" has both a severe and a mild connotation. If you consider it from a severe perspective, the phrase can be as strict sounding as the stick applied to zazen practitioners to keep them concentrated, while if you try accepting it from a moderate perspective, it can have a calming effect, as if you were nestled in silk floss. It appears that truly valuable teachings have a way of nurturing us to some degree or other whether we consider them sternly or perceive them mildly.

If we consider that the spirit of chadō that is summed up in Rikyū's "Harmony, Respect, Purity, Tranquility" is comparable to the trunk of a tree, then the sensibilities of the successive generations of head masters and chanoyu enthusiasts have induced the growth of branches and leaves according to their era. Branches and leaves will only sprout if a tree trunk is solid, and, as you know, a wide range of branches and leaves — the training exercises known as the *shichijishiki*, the *ryūrei* style of tea-making, the Gakkō Chadō program for providing school students with chadō education, the Seinenbu youth division, and the mission of Urasenke to share chadō overseas, for example — have sprung forth from that trunk having its basis in "Harmony, Respect, Purity, Tranquility." None of these branches and leaves came about forcibly, but developed naturally, according to how the sunlight and wind struck the tree at the time; in other words, they developed in answer to the needs of that particular era.

After I took over as the current head of Urasenke, the first concrete item that I created was the Washin-dana, in that I sensed the need for something like this in our contemporary world. The Washin-dana is a tea-making table designed to enable people to easily enjoy chanoyu in a Western-style room, and it can double as a corner accent table or the like. The next thing that I advanced was a method of making tea sitting cross-legged. It is difficult nowadays to have a tatami-floored room, and inasmuch as people mainly live in carpeted or wood-floored spaces, it is not easy for them to have a ro (sunken hearth) built into the floor or to burn real charcoal under the kettle. Many people in this situation nevertheless want to enjoy chadō. The biggest problem, however, is that sitting in the seiza sitting position is prohibitive unless it is on tatami. I thought long and hard if there weren't some way to enjoy chadō sitting comfortably, and finally came up with the *zarei* (lit., "seated decorum") tea-making method. This method was conceptualized to allow for the making of tea without imposing stress on the legs. This may have tended to take people by surprise, but already in the Edo period (1600–1867) the *Irekodate* tea-making method had been devised for youngsters and people with leg impairments.

This does not change the fact, of course, that the study of chanoyu is a means of developing oneself through training. However, it is best for those who aim to devote themselves to this training if they have choices of approaches depending upon their living environment. What is important is how a person moves forward after once experiencing chanoyu. The proper path to follow, no matter the entryway from which one enters onto it, is the one great path of "Harmony, Respect, Purity, Tranquility"; in other words, the proper path is that which connects to the tree trunk.

今日庵

Konnichian (exterior south side)
The Konnichian (Hut of This Day), located deep within the inner roji at the historical Urasenke estate, is Urasenke's iconic tea room. Genpaku Sōtan, grandson of Sen Rikyū, built it as his retirement retreat. The entire Urasenke estate is called Konnichian from the name of this tea room.

今日庵

Konnichian (interior facing the south side)

The Konnichian is a 'thatched hut' (*sōan*) style tea room of the smallest practical size; only one full tatami for guests and a *daime*-size tatami for the host's tea-making. A wall serves as the place to hang a scroll or flowers, and in this and all other ways, the room's structural elements have been pared down as far as possible, creating a space that speaks clearly of the wabi aesthetic.

The Urasenke Family Lineage

NOTE: The calendar utilized in pre-Meiji Japan was a lunar calendar, and years were referred to in terms of the era name and year during that era. Sen Rikyū is said to have died on the 28th day of the 2nd month in the 19th year of the Tenshō era. The day of the occurrence would have been the 21st day of April, 1591, according to the Gregorian calendar.

Founder **Rikyū Sōeki** (1522–91)

初祖 利休宗易

The founder of the chadō legacy of the Sen family is usually known to us by the name Sen Rikyū. Born in the port city of Sakai in the old province of Izumi, present-day Osaka prefecture, the name he used as a child was Yoshirō, and the family into which he was born belonged to the guild of well-to-do warehouse owners. He was commonly known during most of his life as Sōeki. Other names which he used were Hōsensai and Rikyū.

When seventeen, he began learning chanoyu in Sakai under a chanoyu devotee named Kitamuki Dōchin, and later he received instruction from a wealthy merchant of Sakai named Takeno Jōō, who was an early proponent of the wabi aesthetic in chanoyu. His first Zen teacher in Sakai was the priest Dairin Sōtō, who gave him the Buddhist name Sōeki, and after Dairin's demise, he became a Zen student of Dairin's successor, the priest Shōrei Sōkin.

Sōeki served as a chanoyu expert for the hegemon Oda Nobunaga, and, after the Honnōji Incident of the 2nd day of the 6th month of 1582, wherein Nobunaga was attacked at Honnōji temple in Kyoto and died, Sōeki entered the service of Nobunaga's avenger and successor, Toyotomi Hideyoshi. In 1585, he was bestowed with the Buddhist lay name and title, Rikyū Koji, so that he could assist Hideyoshi in serving tea at the Imperial Palace in celebration of Hideyoshi's new position of Kanpaku, or Regent to the reigning emperor. Through the urging of the priest Kokei Sōchin of Daitokuji's Sōken'in temple, he contributed the upper story (Kinmōkaku) of the main temple gate of the Daitokuji monastery compound. Not long thereafter, and for reasons which remain uncertain, he was ordered to commit ritual suicide by Hideyoshi. He carried out this order on the 28th day of the 2nd month, Tenshō 19 (1591), at his residence located in the special Juraku quarters attached to Hideyoshi's Jurakudai palace in Kyoto.

It was during his late years that Sen Rikyū consummated his philosophy concerning the practice of chanoyu, and effectively transformed the enjoyment of chanoyu into a profound 'way' or approach to life. He began to use very tiny, rustic tea rooms. His wabi philosophy and creativity found expression in his development and use of Raku tea bowls, his creation of flower containers, tea scoops, and lid rests made of bamboo, and his use of ordinary objects from everyday life, which he adapted and used in new ways for chadō.

Rikyū's grave is located at Jukōin temple within the Daitokuji monastery compound in Kyoto, as are the ancestral graves of all the Kyoto Sen family. The memorial for Rikyū is annually observed at Urasenke Konnichian on March 28.

2nd Generation Shōan Sōjun (1546–1614)

Shōan was the son of Rikyū's second wife, Sōon, and married a daughter of Rikyū's who is believed to have been called Okame. He was commonly known by the names Shirōzaemon and Sōjun, and he also went by the byname Shōan. Together with Rikyū and Rikyū's true son Dōan, who was his same age, he served as one of Toyotomi Hideyoshi's chanoyu experts. After Rikyū's death, he sought shelter in Aizu-Wakamatsu with Gamō Ujisato, a feudal lord and military commander who had been one of Rikyū's disciples. Through the intercession of Gamō and Tokugawa Ieyasu, who later became the first generalissimo of the Tokugawa government, Shōan received Hideyoshi's pardon and returned to Kyoto, where he reconstructed Rikyū's tea room named Fushin'an at the family's house in front of Honpōji temple. He soon turned the headship of the house over to his son, Sen Rikyū's grandson, and thereafter quietly supported him from a distance.

3rd Generation Genpaku Sōtan (1578–1658)

Rikyū's grandson Shūri, son of Shōan and Rikyū's daughter Okame, was born in Sakai on the 1st day of the 1st month, 1578. He was commonly known by the name Sōtan, but also used the bynames Genpaku, Genshuku, Totsutotsusai, Fushin'an, Konnichian, Totsusai, and Kan'un. When he was around the age of ten, his grandfather, Rikyū, had him become an acolyte under the priest Shun'oku Sōen at Sangen'in temple in the Daitokuji monastery compound in Kyoto.

Following the death of Rikyū and Shōan's eventual return to the family's house in Kyoto, Sōtan returned to secular life and, at the age of eighteen, became the head of the house. Shunning offers to serve in public office, he led an austere life dedicated to the practice of the wabi aesthetic in accordance with his belief that the essence of chadō and Zen are the same. As for his children, however, he found government positions for three of his four sons, enabling them each to become self-sufficient.

In 1646, Sōtan announced that he would retire, and he had the third of his four sons, Kōshin Sōsa (1613–72), succeed as head of the house. At this time, he built a tiny retirement tea hut for himself at the back of the property, naming it "Konnichian." Later, he added a four-and-a-half tatami tea room named Yūin, and an eight tatami reception room named Kan'untei. By and by, his fourth son inherited this property. Meanwhile, his second son, Ichio Sōshū (1605–75), established himself on Mushakōji street, and built his own tea house there. In time, the three consequent Sen households in Kyoto respectively became known as the Omotesenke, Urasenke, and Mushakōjisenke.

Sōtan died on the 19th day of the 12th month, 1658. At Urasenke Konnichian, his memorial is annually observed on November 19.

4th Generation Sensō Sōshitsu (1622–97)

The childhood name of Sōtan's fourth son was Chōkichirō. At first he aspired to become a physician, but following the demise of his mentor physician, Noma Gentaku, he returned to his family and took up chadō as his lifework. During his apprenticeship under Gentaku, he was known as Genshitsu, and then he altered this to Sōshitsu. Other names which he used were Sensō and Rōgetsuan.

Sensō served as chadō accouterment magistrate (*chadōgu bugyō*) for Maeda Toshitsune, lord of the Kaga domain (present-day Ishikawa and Toyama prefectures), and helped to establish a flourishing tea culture in the region. He took the potter Chōzaemon, who worked under Raku Ichinyū, the fourth generation in the Raku line, to Kaga, where Chōzaemon established the Ōhi kiln to produce tea ceramics. Sensō also encouraged Miyazaki Kanchi to establish a foundry to cast tea kettles there.

In the early 1670s, his brothers Kōshin and Ichio passed away, leaving him as the eldest head of the three families. In that capacity, he held the important thirteenth memorial anniversary for his father and, in 1690, the centennial memorial for Rikyū. After this, he retired from his position in Kaga and returned to Kyoto. At the family estate, he supervised the construction of a Rikyū Onsodō (Shrine of the Honorable Ancestor, Rikyū), and had features of the architecture seen in Kaga incorporated into its design.

5th Generation Fukyūsai Jōsō (1673–1704)

Senso's first son and successor was born in Kaga and was known in childhood as Yosaburō. In adulthood, he went by the names Sōan as well as Sōshitsu, initiating the tradition for the generations in his family line, the Urasenke line, to usually adopt the name Sōshitsu which was first used by his father. Other bynames which he used were Jōsō and Fukyūsai.

Fukyūsai succeeded his father as chadō magistrate for the Maeda daimyō of Kaga, headquartered at Kanazawa Castle, and later, through the latter's recommendation, he became chadō magistrate for the Iyo Hisamatsu daimyō family, who occupied Matsuyama Castle (in present-day Ehime prefecture on the island of Shikoku). Unfortunately, he was only thirty-two when he died.

6th Generation Rikkansai Taisō (1694–1726)

The eldest son of Fukyūsai Jōsō had the childhood name Masakichirō, and was known in adulthood as Sōan. He also used the bynames Rikkansai and Taisō. Because of his father's early death, he succeeded as the sixth head of Urasenke when he was only eleven years old. He received his chadō training from Kakukakusai Gensō (1678–1730), the sixth head of Omotesenke, among others. His Zen training was under Daitokuji's Daishin Gitō (1657–1730), and he studied Confucianism under the guidance of the Confucian scholar, Itō Tōgai (1670–1736). Carrying on his father's appointment, he served as head of chanoyu affairs for the Iyo Hisamatsu daimyō family. He was at the Edo (modern-day Tokyo) residence of the Hisamatsu clan when, unfortunately, he fell ill and his life of thirty-three years ended.

7th Generation Saisaisai Chikusō (1709–33)

After Rikkansai's untimely death, the second son of Omotesenke's Kakukakusai Gensō was pressed into service to become the seventh head of Urasenke. Called Masanosuke as a child, he was later known as Sōken, and used the bynames Saisaisai and Chikusō. Together with his elder brother, who later became the seventh-generation head of Omotesenke, he received guidance from his father, Kakukakusai. Unfortunately, however, he passed away at the age of twenty-five, leaving no offspring.

8th Generation Yūgensai Ittō (1719–71)

Left without an heir, the Urasenke household again looked to the Omotesenke house for a successor. Chikusō's younger brother, Tōichirō, who was the third son of Kakukakusai Gensō, was selected to become the eighth-generation head of Urasenke. As the Urasenke head master, he was known as Sōshitsu. He also used the bynames Yūgensai, Ittō, Futsufutsuken, and Baigandō. He served the Iyo Hisamatsu daimyō family and also the Hachisuka family of Awa (present-day Tokushima).

Around this era, chanoyu tended to be considered a sort of artistic amusement. Amid this trend, Ittō underwent Zen training at Daitokuji temple under the guidance of the priest Dairyū Sōjō, and with his brother Joshinsai Tennen (1705–51), who had become the seventh-generation head of Omotesenke, received instruction from the priest Mugaku Sōen of Daitokuji, leading to their creation of the *shichijishiki* (seven training exercises) based on words in the *Hekiganroku* (Blue Cliff Record) about the seven things a priest should have on his person. Other notable accomplishments of Yūgensai include his restoration work on the Urasenke property, and his writing of a work entitled *Hama no Masago* (Sand on the Beach), which explained about the handling of chanoyu implements and was a forerunner as a chanoyu procedural guidebook.

9th Generation Fukensai Sekiō (1746–1801)

The firstborn son of Yūgensai, named Kumesaburō at birth, succeeded Yūgensai as the ninth-generation head of Urasenke. He was known as Genshitsu, and also used the bynames Fukensai, Sekiō, and Kan'un. He studied Japanese and Chinese literature under the tutelage of the nobleman Hino Sukeki, and had close relationships with linked-verse poet Satomura Shōitsu and Tosa Mitsusada, head painter of the atelier providing art pieces to the Edo shogunate.

His major accomplishments were to restore the Urasenke property after Kyoto's great fire of 1788, in time to hold the bicentennial memorial observance for Rikyū in 1790.

Fukensai altogether had three sons, the third of whom was twenty-five years younger than the first. This third son was adopted by the eighth-generation head of the Mushakoji-senke line of the Sen family, Ittotsusai Kyūō (1763–1838), and became the ninth head of that line, who is known as Kōkōsai Nin'ō (1795–1835).

10th Generation Nintokusai Hakusō (1770–1826)

Fukensai's eldest son became the tenth in the Urasenke line at the age of thirty-two. He was known as Sōshitsu, and used the bynames Nintokusai and Hakusō. He was successor to the role of head of chanoyu affairs for the Iyo Hisamatsu daimyō family. He had close connections not only with daimyō but also merchants and others in Nagasaki on the island of Kyushu, and Matsusaka in Mie Prefecture.

Nintokusai's wife was from the long-standing Zetsu family of Kibune in northern Kyoto. She received chadō training under Fukensai, and was known as Shōshitsu Sōkō. The first son born between Nintokusai and Sōkō died at the age of twenty-six, and although they had five other boy children, all died before reaching adulthood. Of their two daughters who survived, the elder, named Machi, was born in 1811.

11th Generation Gengensai Seichū (1810–77)

In 1819, when Nintokusai was fifty, he adopted a boy to be raised as his heir and to become his daughter Machi's husband. The boy was the fifth son of the lord Matsudaira Noritomo of the Okudono territory in Mikawa Province (part of present Aichi prefecture), who held the title of Captain of the Wardrobe Sewing Bureau (*Nuidono-no-kami*). As a child he was called Chiyomatsu, and later in life he went by the names Genshitsu and Sōshitsu. He also used the bynames Gengensai, Seichū, Fubō, Kyohakusai, and Kan'un. He became the eleventh-generation head of Urasenke when he was only sixteen, due to the death of Nintokusai. His adoptive mother, Shōshitsu Sōkō (d. 1844), provided family guidance after Nintokusai's death.

In preparation for the two hundred and fiftieth memorial observance for Rikyū in 1840, Gengensai oversaw several new additions to the Urasenke property, including the Kabutomon "helmet gate," the front entrance area of the house, and the rooms named Totsutotsusai, Dairo-no-ma, Hōsensai, and Ryūseiken. In 1866, he made an offering of tea to the Imperial Family, which he commemorated by restoring the *Wakin-date* tea-making method and making it available for Urasenke tea practitioners to study. He also designed several new temae, including tea-making methods for portable chanoyu sets (*chabako*) and the *ryūrei* style of tea-making which employs tables and stools.

Between Gengensai and Machi, there was born one boy. Tragically, however, the boy died at the age of sixteen. Consequently, when Gengensai was past sixty, he had his daughter Yuka marry a young man who would be his successor.

12th Generation Yūmyōsai Jikisō (1852–1917)

Yūmyōsai was born into the prominent Suminokura family of Kyoto. He married Gengensai's daughter Yuka (1859–1916) in 1871, at which point he was adopted into the Urasenke family. He was known as Genshitsu, and used the bynames Jikisō, Yūken, and Yūmyōsai. In 1885, Yūmyōsai, at the age of thirty-four, turned the headship of the house over to his eldest son and retired to Myōkian temple in Yamazaki. Later, he moved to various locations, including Sakai, and worked to revive interest in chadō, which, because of the changes brought on by the Meiji Restoration, had suffered a loss in popularity and support. Yuka, who is known as Shinseiin, worked actively to have chadō included in the curriculum of the newly established girls' secondary schools.

13th Generation Ennōsai Tetchū (1872–1924) 十三代 圓能斎鉄中

The firstborn son of Yūmyōsai and Yuka, Komakichi, became the head of Urasenke at the age of fourteen. He went by the name Sōshitsu, and also used the bynames Ennōsai, Tetchū, Tairyūken, Kan'un, and Shichienshi. After his marriage in 1889, he and his wife lived for a while in Japan's new capital, Tokyo, to encourage Urasenke followers there. Returning to Kyoto, in 1907 Ennōsai held the 250th memorial observance for Sen Sōtan, and as a commemorative project for that, he began publishing the *Konnichian Geppō* (Konnichian Monthly Bulletin), the forerunner of today's *Tankō Zasshi* magazine. Among his many accomplishments, he also initiated the annual "summer intensive seminar" (*kaki-kōshūkai*) held at Urasenke headquarters, designed such temae as *Bonryaku* and *Koicha Kakufukudate* (the preparation of single servings of *koicha*), and revived the *Furo Nagashidate* method of temae in which the temae is conducted diagonally facing the guests, much like when conducting a ro temae.

14th Generation Mugensai Sekisō (1893–1964) 十四代 無限斎碩叟

Ennōsai's first son, Masanosuke, was born in Tokyo in 1893. He went by the names Eise, Sōshuku, and Sōshitsu. He also used the bynames Genkuken, Genkusai, Tantansai, Sekisō, Baishian, and Mugensai. He graduated from Dōshisha University in Kyoto and, in 1924, became the fourteenth-generation head of Urasenke at the age of thirty-two. He took Buddhist vows under Abbot Maruyama Denne of Daitokuji temple, from whom he received the name Mugensai. Later, a member of the aristocratic Kujō family gave him the name Tantansai, by which he is commonly known.

Mugensai presented tea to Empress Teimei at Daitokuji temple in 1925, which was the first of his many opportunities to present tea to members of the Imperial Family, including Emperor Taishō's eldest son, Crown Prince Akihito, and second son, Prince Chichibu. He also revived the custom of conducting tea offerings and tea dedications at shrines and temples. To normalize the universal practice of Urasenke chadō, Mugensai established the Tankōkai association. Also, he established the International Chadō Culture Foundation, to promote chadō outside Japan and encourage international cultural exchange. He was the first person in the chadō world to be awarded a medal from the Emperor of Japan; the Order of the Rising Sun, Gold Rays with Neck Ribbon. He went on later to receive the Medal of Honor with Blue Ribbon as well as the Medal of Honor with Purple Ribbon.

On September 7, 1964, Mugensai passed away during a business trip to Hokkaido. His memorial is annually observed at Urasenke Konnichian on July 5, jointly with that for Gengensai and Ennōsai.

15th Generation Hōunsai Hansō (1923–) 十五代 鵬雲斎汎叟

Mugensai's first son, named Masaoki at birth, was born on April 19, 1923. He has had the names Sōkō, Sōshitsu, and Genshitsu. His bynames include Hōunsai, Genshū, Kyoshin, and Hansō. After serving in the air force division of the Japanese navy during WWII, he completed his temporarily interrupted university education at Dōshisha University, Kyoto, graduating from the Faculty of Economics. He undertook Zen training and took the Buddhist tonsure under Gotō Zuigan of Daitokuji temple, and was confirmed as Urasenke heir apparent (*wakasōshō*; lit., "young master") in 1950. He succeeded as the fifteenth-generation head of Urasenke in 1964, upon his father's death.

Hōunsai has left a legacy of overseas Tankōkai associations and has donated tea houses and tea rooms worldwide. He has proposed that chadō is rooted in the combination of the way/principle (*dō*), study/learning (*gaku*), and practice/practical skill (*jitsu*). He has personally been a dedicated student of the history and culture of tea, and holds a Ph.D. from Nankai University, China, awarded to him in 1991 for his successful defense of his thesis concerning the influence of the *Cha Jing*, by Lu Yu (8th c.) on the development of Japan's chadō culture, and a Litt.D. from Chung-Ang University, Korea, awarded to him in 2008.

He was the first in the chadō world to be awarded the Order of Culture by the Emperor of Japan, and has been awarded many other decorations and merits from Japan and countries across the world. In 2002, he turned the headship of Urasenke over to his son, Zabōsai, and took the name Genshitsu, but he continues to actively promote his goal, capsulized in the phrase, "Peacefulness through a bowl of tea," by sharing chadō internationally.

16th Generation Zabōsai Genmoku (1956–)

十六代 坐忘斎玄黙

Zabōsai was born on June 7, 1956, as Hōunsai's first son. His birth name was Masayuki. He has had the names Sōshi and Sōshitsu, and his bynames include Zabōsai and Genmoku. He took the Buddhist tonsure under Nakamura Sojun of Daitokuji temple, and was confirmed as Urasenke heir apparent in 1982. In 2002, he succeeded as the sixteenth-generation head of Urasenke, and took the name Sōshitsu. The following year, he held the 300th memorial observance for the fifth head of Urasenke, Fukyūsai Jōsō; in 2007, the 350th memorial observance for the grandson of Sen Rikyū, Genpaku Sōtan; and in 2016, the 100th memorial observance for the twelfth head of Urasenke, Yūmyōsai Jikisō.

Quick Chart of the Lineage

Founder	2nd Generation	3rd Generation	4th Generation
Rikyū Sōeki	Shōan Sōjun	Genpaku Sōtan	Sensō Sōshitsu

5th Generation	6th Generation	7th Generation	8th Generation
Fukyūsai Jōsō	Rikkansai Taisō	Saisaisai Chikusō	Yūgensai Ittō

9th Generation	10th Generation	11th Generation	12th Generation
Fukensai Sekiō	Nintokusai Hakusō	Gengensai Seichū	Yūmyōsai Jikisō

13th Generation	14th Generation	15th Generation	16th Generation
Ennōsai Tetchū	Mugensai Sekisō (Tantansai)	Hōunsai Hansō	Zabōsai Genmoku

Monogram Signatures (*kaō*) of the Urasenke Lineage

Founder Rikyū Sōeki	2nd Generation Shōan Sōjun	3rd Generation Genpaku Sōtan	4th Generation Sensō Sōshitsu

5th Generation Fukyūsai Jōsō	6th Generation Rikkansai Taisō	7th Generation Saisaisai Chikusō	8th Generation Yūgensai Ittō

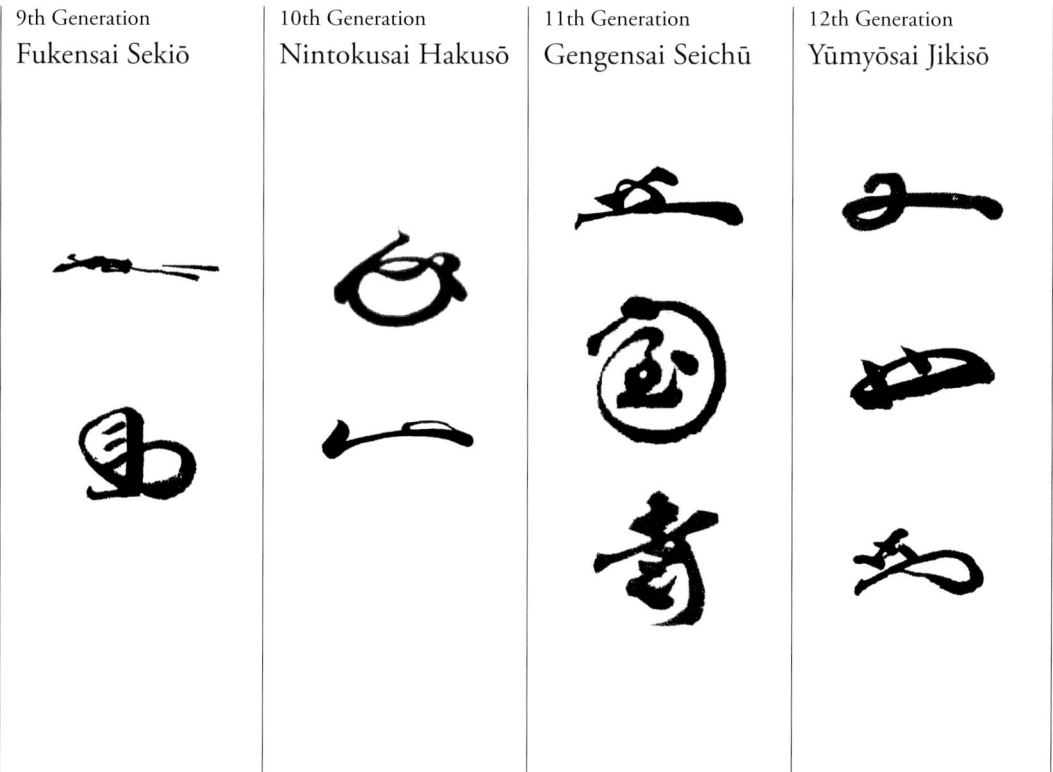

9th Generation
Fukensai Sekiō

10th Generation
Nintokusai Hakusō

11th Generation
Gengensai Seichū

12th Generation
Yūmyōsai Jikisō

13th Generation
Ennōsai Tetchū

14th Generation
Mugensai Sekisō
 (Tantansai)

15th Generation
Hōunsai Hansō

16th Generation
Zabōsai Genmoku

Before Beginning to Take Lessons

Personal Items Required for Practicing Chadō

There are several items which you must be prepared with to practice chadō. They include a particular type of sensu (folding fan), a fukusa, a kobukusa, a packet of special pocket paper called kaishi, a sweets pick called yōji, contained in a holder for it, and a clutch referred to as a fukusabasami, in which to keep these items. These are basic items which are necessary to have with you not only for taking chadō lessons, but also, as you continue your involvement with chadō, for participating in chadō functions of any sort. Between men and women, there are size and/or color differences for the sensu, fukusa, kaishi paper, and the fukusabasami clutch. These items can be found and assembled into a full set at shops that handle implements for use in chadō.

One other item that is good to be prepared with and keep in your fukusabasami clutch is a small linen wiping cloth called kojakin, contained in a case for it, called kojakin-ire.

Aside from the items kept in the fukusabasami clutch, always be prepared with a clean change of tabi or socks and a thin hand towel or handkerchief.

1. Sensu
2. Fukusa
3. Kobukusa
4. Kaishi
5. Yōji in holder
6. Fukusabasami
7. Kojakin-ire

How to Dress

Kimono is the standard attire anywhere that chadō is the focus of the activity, and being dressed in kimono is the premise for many of the movements in chadō. To acculture yourself to chadō, it is therefore conducive to wear kimono at your practice sessions. However, it is becoming more and more common for people to wear western clothes at their chadō practice sessions. Whether in western clothes or kimono, in chadō it is important to strive for neatness and cleanliness, and to be dressed in a manner which is not distracting or disturbing to others.

Chadō practice sessions are to be undertaken with mind and body in purified condition. Therefore, before entering the tea room, you should remove the socks or tabi that you had on as you came to your practice session and change into a fresh pair. Also, to avoid inadvertently causing damage to the treasured implements handled in chadō, accessories such as rings and bracelets, as well as wristwatches, are removed.

Sensu	Folding fan. This important item is placed in front of yourself as a sign of respect when expressing greetings with the teacher or host and fellow guests, and when, as a guest, you inspect the scroll and other articles in the alcove and at the place for the temae. When seated on the floor in a conventional tea room as a guest, it lies at rest behind you. The fans for women are 5 *sun* (approx.15 cm) in length, and normally are made of plain white bamboo or wood with a lacquer finish. The fans for men are 6 *sun* (approx.18 cm) in length, and are commonly made of plain white bamboo or wood with a solid black finish.
Fukusa	Silk purifying cloth. Among its uses, the fukusa most notably is utilized during the temae to purify certain implements. Women use crimson or scarlet fukusa, and men use purple. The fukusa is the symbol of the host (hosting side), and is worn whenever serving tea.
Kobukusa	Square of fine fabric. Both host and guest make use of this for many purposes, often having to do with the display and handling of valuable articles.
Kaishi	Pocket paper. The paper is predominantly used by the guest to set the confection on, but it can be put to use for various other purposes. Kaishi for women are about 175 mm x 145 mm, and that for men are about 206 mm x 175 mm. Host and guests alike should always keep a packet of this paper on them.
Yōji	Sweets pick. There is a wide range of styles of yōji, including ones made of wood, plastic, or metal, and they generally have their own holder. This little implement is used to cut and to eat the omogashi (moist confection). It is usually kept in the fold of the packet of kaishi.
Fukusabasami	Clutch in which to keep these items. When wearing kimono, the personal items which will be required are basically kept in the kimono when inside the tea room, and the fukusabasami is left outside. Guests wearing western clothes carry in the fukusabasami which contains the items.
Kojakin and Kojakin-ire	Small wiping cloth and the case for it. The kojakin is like a standard chakin, but smaller in both length and width. When guests share a bowl of koicha, they each in turn use a damp kojakin to wipe the part of the chawan rim from where they drank. The case for it has waterproof lining, to keep your kimono or fukusabasami from getting wet or soiled from the prepared and then used kojakin.
Clean Change of Tabi or Socks	Especially in chadō, importance is placed on having cleanly tabi or socks covering the feet; tabi in the case of kimono, and socks in the case of western clothes. White is the standard color. You should be prepared with a clean pair to change into before entering the chadō venue.
Hand Towel or Handkerchief	Hands are rinsed and purified before entering a tea room. You should be prepared with your own towel or handkerchief for drying your hands at this time.

Fundamental Techniques

Mannerly Deportment
Temae Fundamentals

Mannerly Deportment

Before delving into the temae methods, it is important to become accustomed to the proper posture and standards of mannerly deportment which form their base. Chadō lessons are a means to learn how to carry yourself in a becoming and natural manner.

The standing position

Men: Let your arms hang down at your sides, slightly away from your body as though holding an invisible egg under each armpit. Your hands should be balled into a very loose fist-like position, with the tip of the thumb and forefinger touching.

Women: Let your arms hang down naturally with shoulders relaxed. Your hands should rest over your thighs and be relaxed, with fingers kept together.

Standing and Walking

First, stand up straight, feet together, with chin pulled in slightly. Arms should be placed as shown above. Without tilting forward and backward as you do so, walk while breathing calmly. Note the sound made as you slide your feet across the tatami. When walking, the arms do not swing back and forth. Men's arms should stay at the sides, as when standing stationary. Likewise, women's hands should stay at rest over the thighs. Taking natural-sized steps, four to a tatami, you can cross a tatami room easily, and at the same time not step on thresholds, the seams between tatami, or the tatami bordering.

The host's sitting position

Hands rest slightly apart on your lap, fingers together.

The guest's sitting position

Hands rest together on your lap, right hand over left, with fingers together. The right hand covers the left hand in a way that the left fingertips are not seen.

Standing up

Let your hands rest slightly apart on your lap, fingers together (1). Bring your weight forward and your feet together, raise your heels, and rest your haunches on your heels (2). Bring your right foot forward slightly (3). Stand up, keeping your back straight. As you stand, let your hands hang down and rest as they would in the standing position (4). Bring your right foot back into alignment with the left (5).

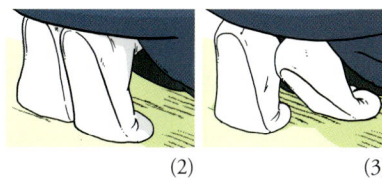

(2)   (3)

Sitting and Standing Up

The standard sitting position in the practice of chadō is *seiza*, the formal "correct sitting" position. It involves sitting with the legs folded underneath the thighs. The back is straight and chin pulled in slightly. The knees are spaced apart: one hand's width for women and two for men. Ideally, the left and right big toes cross while the heels are spread apart, creating a space to rest the buttocks. Hands rest in the lap, with elbows held slightly away from the body. When standing up from *seiza*, try to do so without changing the posture of your upper body, keeping your back straight and chin pulled in slightly. The transitional position between sitting and standing, involving sitting on your heels, is called *kiza*, the "seated while kneeling" position. If you cannot position your feet in *kiza* from tiredness or numbness due to lack of circulation, do not try to stand until your control of your feet has returned.

Bowing from a sitting position

Shin: Make a slow, steady bow deep enough that your palms are placed fully on the floor.

Gyō: Bow less deeply. The fingers are almost fully on the floor with the palms slightly raised.

Sō: The fingertips rest lightly on the floor.

Bowing – the Three Types of Bows

Bows are classified according to their level of formality: *shin* (formal), *gyō* (semi-formal), and *sō* (informal). In the case of any of these, what is as important as the form is that you feel a sense of respect toward the recipient of the bow. To bow, start first in the proper sitting position with back straight and chin pulled in slightly. After making eye contact with the recipient of the bow, lean forward while keeping your back straight. At the same time, let your hands slide forward off your thighs and quietly to the floor. When bending forward to bow and straightening up following the bow, move slowly and conscientiously.

Making a *shin* bow
This is the most gracious way of bowing. It is used when host and guest formally exchange greetings, and is the bow the guest uses when thanking the host for the tea before picking up the tea bowl to drink.

To make a *shin* bow, lower your upper body while letting your hands slide forward to the floor. Think of bringing your chest and knees close together; do not just bow your head. The bow is deep enough that the palms and fingers lie flat on the floor.

Bowing from a standing position

Shin: The hands come to rest at the knees.

Gyō: The hands come to rest above the knees.

Sō: The body leans forward only slightly.

Making a *gyō* bow
The *gyō* bow is made just as a *shin* bow, but is not quite as deep. Keeping your back and neck straight, lean forward to the point that your fingers touch the floor but palms do not. This semi-formal bow is used, for instance, at times of interaction between guests.

Making a *sō* bow
For the *sō* bow, lean forward only slightly, until the tips of your fingers reach the floor. The host uses this type of bow when interacting with the guest while in the midst of conducting the temae.

Bowing from a standing position
The standing bow also has the same *shin*, *gyō*, and *sō* levels of formality. After making eye contact with the recipient of the bow, slowly lean forward from the hips, while letting your hands slide down your thighs. When returning to the upright position, again move slowly and serenely.

    For a *shin* bow, you lean forward until your fingertips reach your knees. For a *gyō* bow, your hands stop above your knees. A *sō* bow is at even less of an angle, and your hands come to rest over your upper thighs.

Opening Fusuma Sliding Doors

Opening and Closing Fusuma Sliding Doors

When opening or closing a fusuma sliding door, it is important not to touch the paper part of the fusuma. Take care only to touch the finger catch and the wooden frame.

To open a closed fusuma, first sit directly in front of it. Using the fingers of the hand closest to the finger catch, slide the fusuma open just enough so that the fingers will fit through (1). The slight opening made serves as a handhold, or *tegakari*.

Put the same hand's extended fingers inside the opening about 24–25 centimeters from the floor (2). The hand not in use should be at rest in your lap this whole time. In a steady movement, push the fusuma open halfway (3).

Let this hand rest on your lap and now extend the other hand to the edge of the fusuma where the first hand was (4), and open the fusuma almost completely (5), leaving just enough of the fusuma protruding to serve as a handhold when closing it.

Closing the fusuma is a reversal of the opening process. First, grasp the frame of the open fusuma with the closer hand at a height of about 24–25 centimeters from the floor (6). In a steady movement, pull the fusuma closed halfway (7). Switch hands (8) and pull the fusuma closed until the back of your hand touches the door jamb (9). Place the fingers of the same hand in the finger catch and close the fusuma completely.

Closing Fusuma Sliding Doors

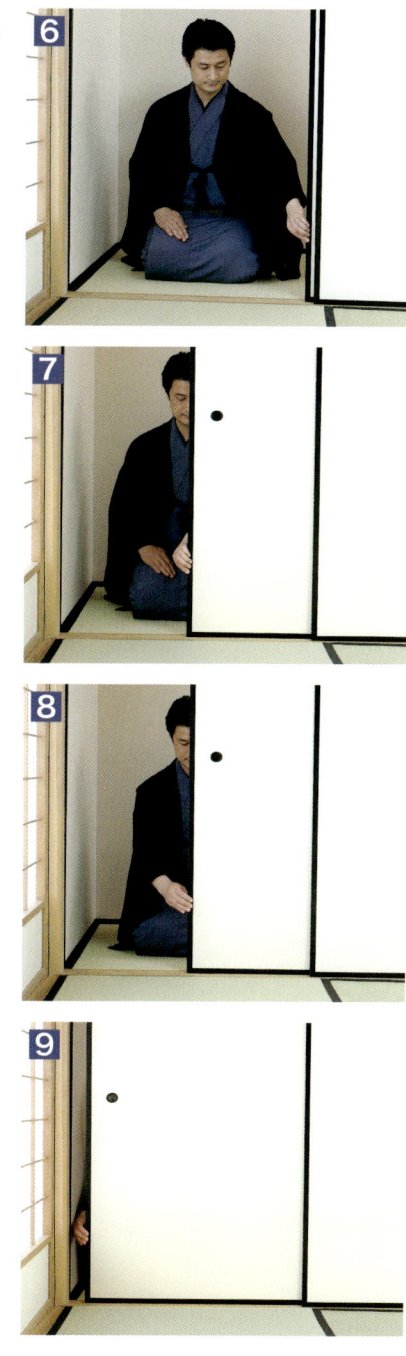

Temae Fundamentals

Here, the basic elements involved in doing temae will be covered. They constitute the foundation for any temae that you will study in the future, and so it is essential that you learn them properly and thoroughly.

Handling the Fukusa

When you are about to conduct a temae or welcome a guest, you put on your fukusa; that is, you hang it from your obi. Having the fukusa in this position is the sign and symbol of being the host, and the very act of putting it on like this gives you a sense of becoming charged and focused. Just as the guest keeps the sensu (folding fan) ready at all times at a tea gathering, the host has the fukusa hung from the obi from when the guests arrive until they leave, and only removes it to handle or purify implements in the course of the temae.

Fukusa may be made of different quality silk fabric such as thick *shioze*, lustrous *habutae*, and mat-weave *nanako*. The fabric is doubled over to make the fukusa. Three edges are sewn together and the remaining edge is the fold, known as the *wasa*. The sides measure about 30 cm. Typically, men use purple fukusa, and women use scarlet or crimson. The measurements of the fukusa are said to have been formulated by Sōon, wife of Sen Rikyū, who wrapped a small medicine container in a cloth of this size, for Rikyū to take with him as he departed for the Odawara battlefield. Rikyū found it easier to use than the smaller sized fukusa used until that time, and so it became the standard fukusa size, while the original, smaller size is said to be preserved in the measurements of the *kobukusa* (literally, "old fukusa").

Fukusasabaki, the folding of the fukusa for use within the temae to purify an implement, is in itself an act of purification. The fukusa is folded prior to its use to purify the natsume, and then folded anew to purify the chashaku. Folding the fukusa anew for each implement gives the sense that the fukusa itself is returned to a pure and new state.

As in bowing, there are *shin* (formal), *gyō* (semi-formal), and *sō* (informal) styles of folding the fukusa. The *sō* style is covered in this "Temae Fundamentals" chapter.

Note that when you are the host and have your fukusa on as such, you put aside your sensu, the sign of being a guest.

Folding the fukusa into eighths and tucking it into your kimono

At those times when you do not have your fukusa on as host or a person on the hosting side, the fukusa will be folded into eighths and either tucked into your kimono or put away in your fukusa-basami. The following instructions show how to fold it into eighths and tuck it into your kimono.

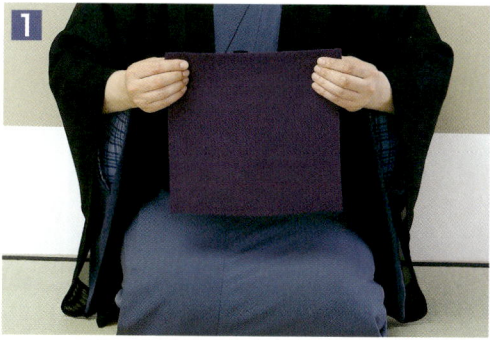

Hold the fukusa open, making certain that the folded edge (*wasa*) is on the right.

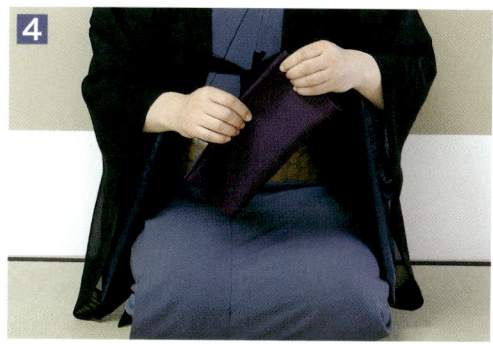

Slide your right hand down the fukusa to hold the next corner.

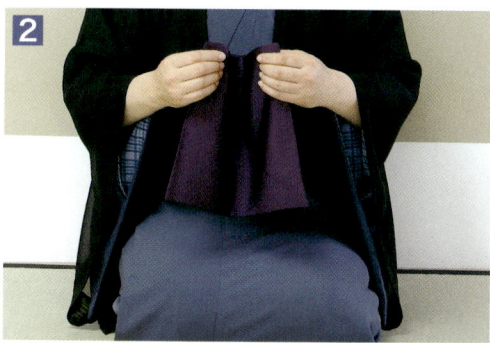

Folding away from yourself, bring the two upper corners of the fukusa together directly in front of you to fold the fukusa in half.

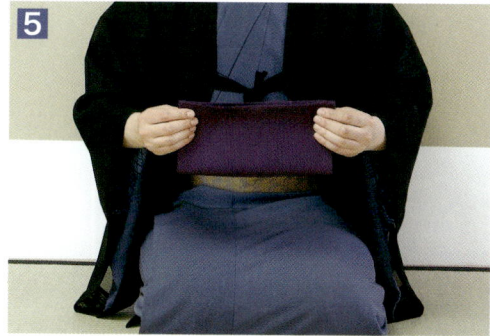

Bring the corners now held by your left and right hands level.

Press your thumbs together to hold the fukusa in place. Reposition your left hand's grasp so that the fingertips press where the thumb did and the thumb presses from where the right thumb is, and bring the right fingers around from the back.

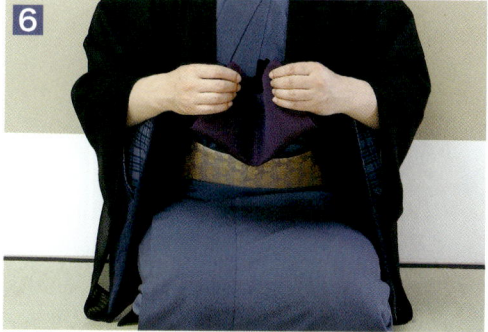

Repeat step 2 to fold the fukusa into quarters, and press your thumbs together to hold the fukusa in place.

As in step 3, reposition your left hand's grasp. Continue as described in steps 3 to 5.

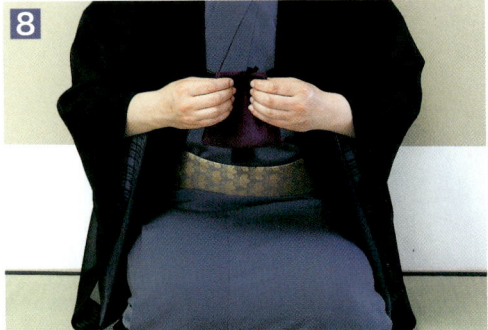

Repeat step 2 to this time fold the fukusa into eighths.

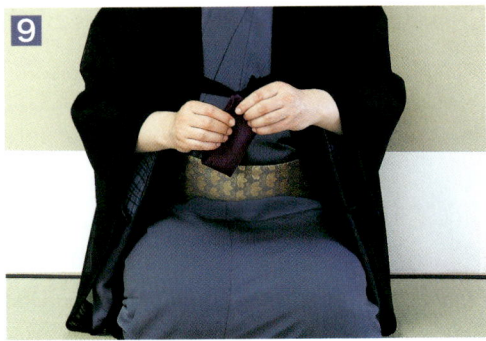

Repeat steps 3 to 5.

Holding the eighthed fukusa with your left hand, reposition your right hand to hold the fukusa from the bottom folded edge with your right fingers toward you and thumb away from you.

Release your left hand.

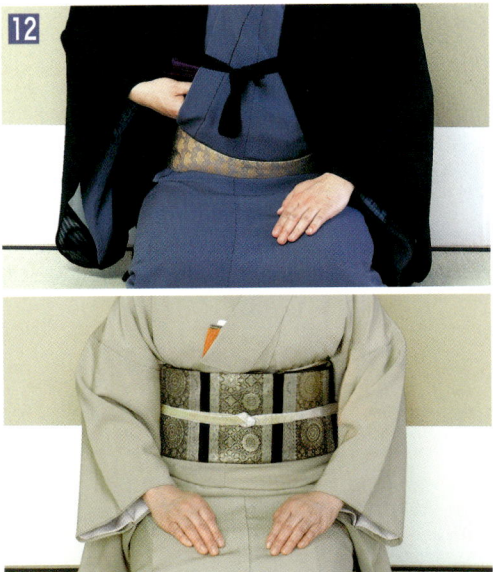

Tuck the fukusa into your kimono.
Because of the differences in male and female kimono design, the fukusa peeks out from women's kimono while the fukusa is fully tucked inside men's kimono.

Hanging the fukusa from your obi

Before beginning host duties, you need to put on your fukusa. This is the starting position of the fukusa when doing temae.

Take the fukusa, folded into eighths as when it is tucked inside your kimono. (See page 34, photo 11) Place it on your left palm, with the fold to the right.

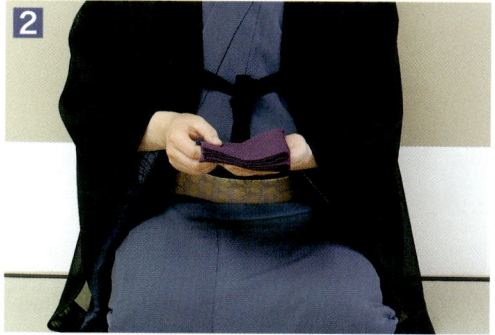

With your right hand, open the fukusa from left to right like opening a Japanese book.

With your right thumb and forefinger, hold the far right corner of the topmost layer.

Let the fukusa fall away from your left hand. A triangle should be formed. With your left hand, hold the fold of the triangle toward the top. Bring your right forefinger together with the other fingers to firmly secure that corner of the triangle.

Slide your left hand, which is clasping the fold of the triangle, down to the bottom corner. Raise the bottom corner to the same level as the corner being held in your right hand.

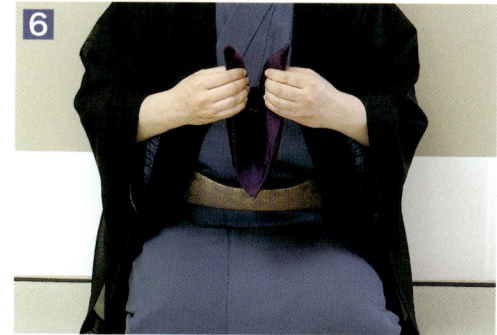

Folding away from yourself, bring the outside corners of the fukusa together in front of you.

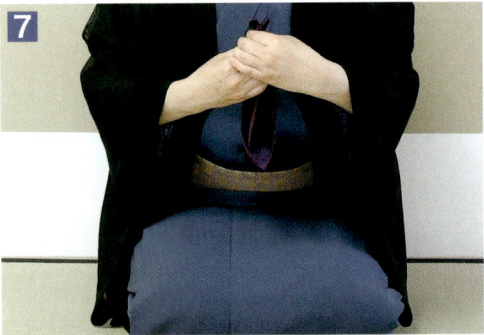

Press your thumbs together, to fold the triangle in half. Bring your left fingers around in order to hold the loose corners together from the outside. Your right thumb and fingers stay as they are, with four fingers inside the newly formed triangle.

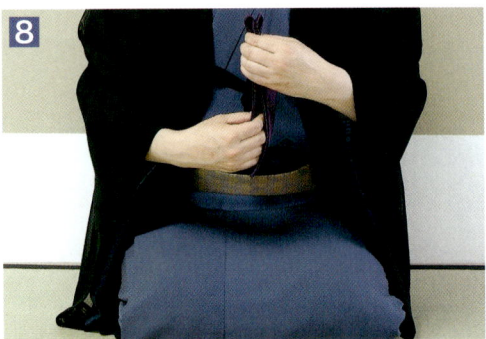

Slide your right hand to the bottom of the triangle.

Rest your right hand on your lap, bring your left hand, which holds the upper corners of the triangularly folded fukusa, to your left side, and tuck those corners into your obi.

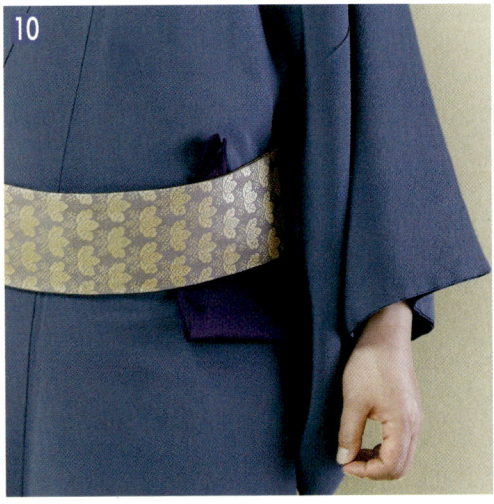

Men, tuck the fukusa in from under your obi, using the four fingers of your left hand to do so. Then, from above the obi, find the corners and pull them up and out, so that the fukusa hangs about one third out from under the obi and is straight.

Women, tuck the fukusa in from above your obi, using the thumb of your left hand to do so. The fukusa should hang about two-thirds out from above the obi and be straight.

Folding the fukusa

The fukusa is folded in a certain way for the purifying of certain tea implements, such as the natsume and the chashaku. The acts of purification, including the fukusa folding in preparation for them, are done with the mental attitude that you are purifying yourself as you purify the implements.

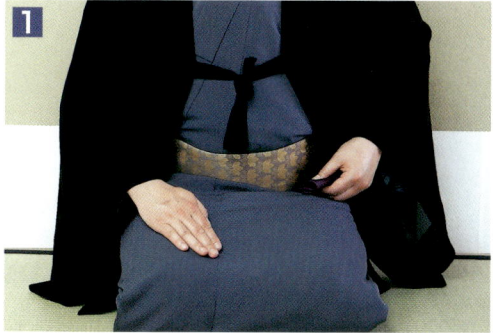

The fukusa is hanging from your obi. Men, pull the bottom with your left hand so that the fukusa is out by about two thirds. (Women, this step does not apply, as the fukusa is already out by about two-thirds.)

Bring the fukusa in front of you. With your right thumb and forefinger, hold the upper right loose corner of the fukusa.

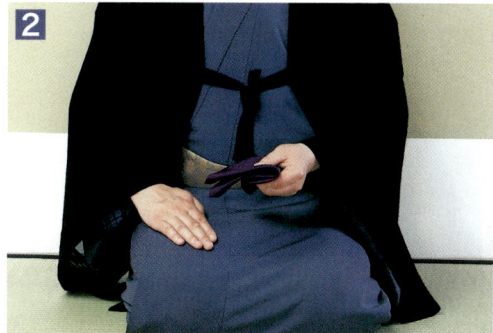

Fold the bottom third of the fukusa inward and under, regrasp the folded portion between your left thumb and fingers, and pull the fukusa free.

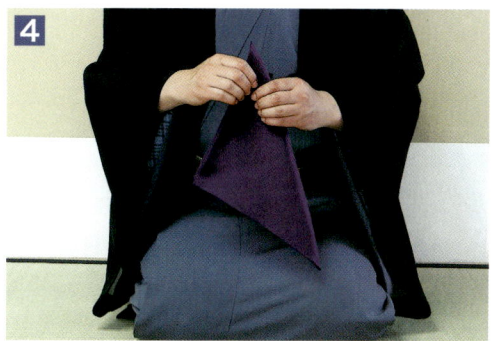

Let the fukusa drop from your left hand and dangle in the large triangle form. Just below your right hand, grasp the fold of the large triangle between your left thumb and fingers.

Women, to remove the fukusa from the obi, fold the bottom third inward and under, regrasp the folded portion between your left thumb and fingers, and pull the fukusa free.

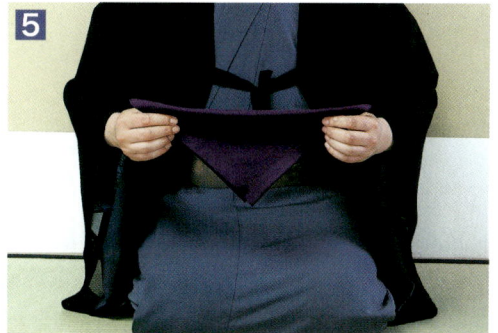

Slide your left thumb and fingers down the fold of the triangle and, as you take the bottom corner, bring that fold so that it is horizontal by raising your left hand and lowering your right.

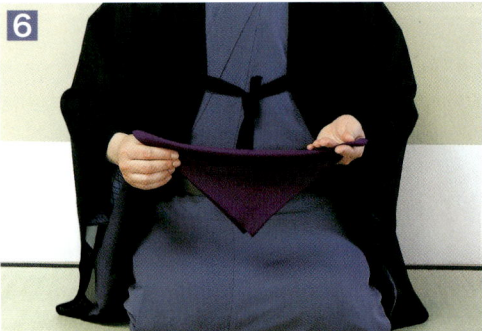

Bring the last three fingers of your left hand around to the front of the fukusa.

With the new fold lightly clasped between your left thumb and fingers, slide your left hand up to about one third from the top, and bend your left fingers to bring the protruding corners of the large triangle inward.

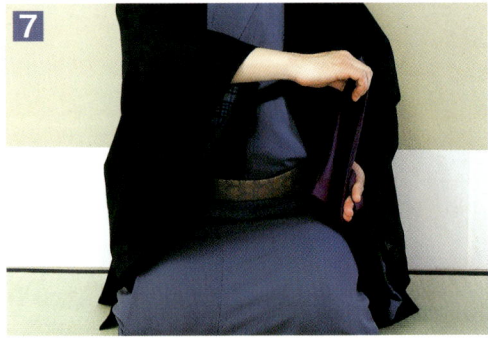

Rotate your left palm so it faces right, while lowering it over the side of your left thigh and extending the fingers. Simultaneously bring your right hand vertically over that while rotating it so that the palm faces downward and your right arm is horizontally aligned with it in front of your body.

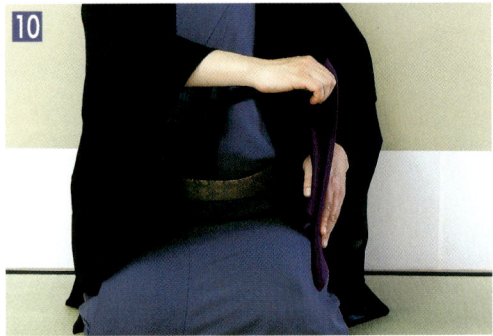

Secure those corners with the thumb, extend the fingers, and slide your left hand down until the thumb comes to about the middle.

Bring your left thumb around, and release the fukusa ends held up by your left forefinger. A large new fold will have formed.

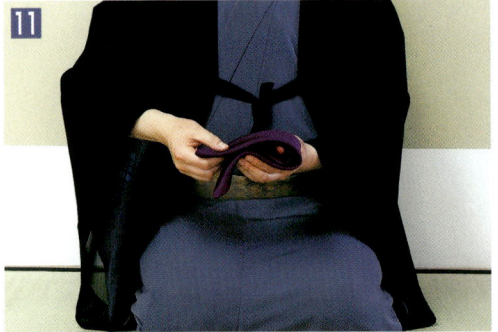

While lowering and rotating your right hand so that the fukusa is folded in half, bring the fukusa so that it is horizontal and in front of you.

Run your right forefinger about half way across the folded fukusa as if drawing the character "一".

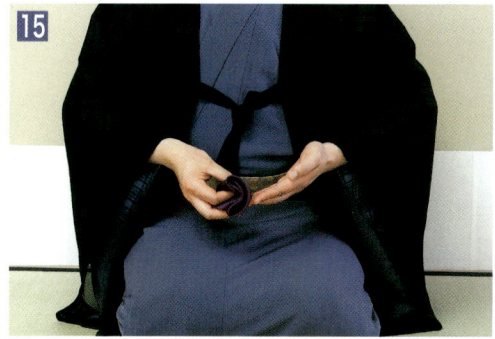

Keeping your right forefinger in the fold, secure the loose bottom fold with the remaining fingers.

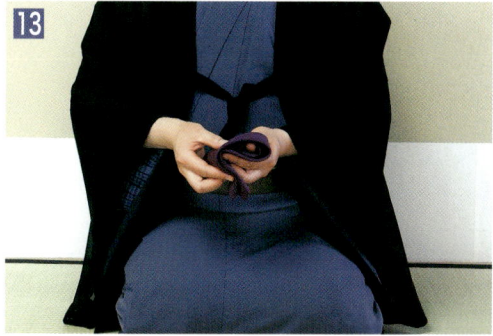

Continuing from movement 12, bend the loose corners of the fukusa under with your right fingers so that the fukusa is folded in half again, clasp that fold between your right thumb and fingers, and release your left hand.

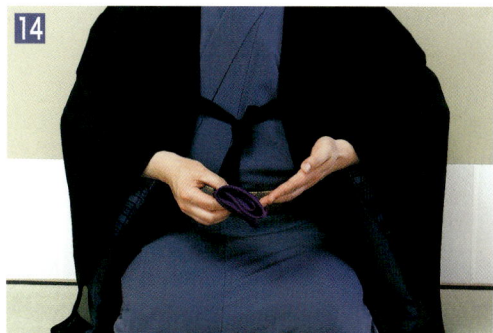

With the extended fingers of your left hand, push the left side of the fukusa under to fold the fukusa in half once again.

While slowly bringing your right forefinger together with the other fingers, lightly rest your right hand, holding the folded-up fukusa, on your right thigh.

Purifying the natsume

A key to conducting this with grace and depth of feeling is, at the point shown in step 7, to slowly slide the fukusa off and straight to the right of the natsume lid, as if one more natsume were there.

Pick up the natsume from its side with your left hand.

Next, wipe the near surface of the lid, left to right.

Bring the natsume directly in front of you over your knees. Use the fukusa to wipe the far surface of the lid, left to right.

Set the folded fukusa on the top of the natsume so that your thumb is facing toward you. Cupping your hand over the fukusa, let the fukusa open one fold over the lid. As the fukusa opens, place your thumb together with your extended fingers to hold the fukusa in place with that hand.

Push the fukusa forward slightly, and then move your right arm from the elbow, thereby turning the hand and fukusa that is under it leftward.

Let your right hand close around the fukusa.

Slowly slide your right hand and the fukusa off the lid and smoothly to the right, as your right hand gradually clutches the fukusa.

Lightly rest your right hand, which is loosely clutching the fukusa, on your right thigh as you place the natsume down in front of your knees with your left hand.

Purifying the natsume for *haiken*

These are the additional steps for purifying the natsume to put it out for the guests' *haiken* — that is, for the guests to examine the natsume closely.

After step 7 of "Purifying the natsume" (page 41), secure the clutched fukusa deep in your right palm with your last two fingers, and with your right thumb and first two fingers, remove the natsume lid.

Place the lid down in front of your knees.

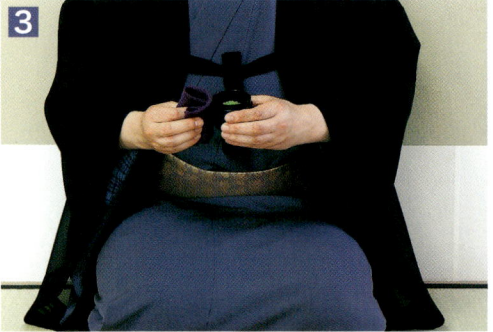

Hold the fukusa against the side of the natsume and regrasp it so that it is folded back into its original folded-up state ("Folding the fukusa" step 16, page 39).

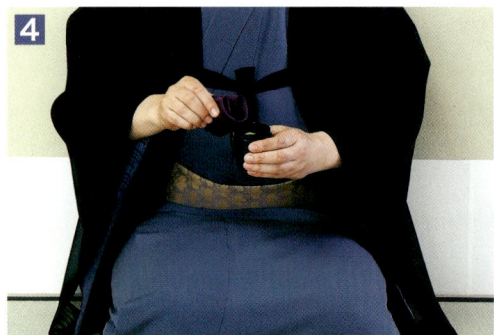

With two left to right motions, wipe the far and near edges of the natsume rim.

Again secure the clutched fukusa deep in your right palm with the last two fingers. Use your right thumb and first two fingers to pick up the natsume lid. Carefully replace the lid on the natsume.

Bring your right forefinger into the middle of the folded fukusa followed by the last three fingers, releasing the fold that is on the far side. Place the fukusa down in front of your knees.

Hold the natsume from above with your right hand and rest it on your left palm.

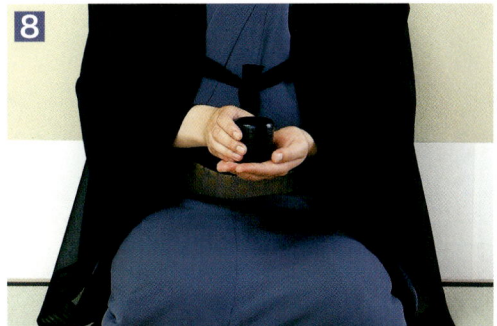

Rotate the natsume two quarter turns clockwise with your right hand, bringing the front to face the opposite direction.

Rehold the natsume from above with your right hand and set it out for the guests' *haiken*.

Purifying the chashaku

Whenever handling a chashaku, it is important to remember to keep it centered in front of your body, and to have it slanting downward somewhat at its scoop end (*kaisaki*). To begin, first the fukusa needs to be in the folded state that it is at step 13 of "Folding the fukusa," and on your left palm.

Take the chashaku with your right hand and set it on the center of the fukusa, scoop facing upward.

Relax the pressure on the fukusa and slide the fukusa back to your right hand, rotating your wrist slightly as your hand returns, so that the thumb and forefinger are pressing to the sides of the chashaku.

Fold the fukusa in half over the chashaku with your left hand, so that your left thumb is on top of the fold, the forefinger is holding from underneath, and the other fingers are aligned with the forefinger.

Slide the fukusa down the chashaku a second time, this time purifying the sides.

Slide the fukusa down to the end of the scoop, purifying the upper and lower surfaces of the chashaku. Your right hand holding the chashaku does not move.

Once the fukusa passes the node (*fushi*), undo the rotation of the wrist so that the hand returns to its original angle as you wipe all the way to the end of the scoop.

Again relax the pressure on the fukusa and slide it back to your right hand, this time without rotating your wrist. Slide the fukusa down the chashaku a third time, as with the first time.

Once the scoop is wiped this third time, relax the left hand's pressure and let the fukusa slide straight forward off the chashaku.

In a smooth, circular motion, bring your left hand which holds the fukusa lightly to rest on your left thigh.

Setting out the natsume and chashaku for *haiken*

The guest may ask to examine the implements used for the temae; that is, to do *haiken* of them. In the case of an usucha temae, it is common practice for the first guest (*shōkyaku*) to request *haiken* of the natsume and chashaku. The host places the purified natsume and chashaku out on the adjacent tatami as seen in this photo. The natsume is put out first, and is placed at a spot on the adjacent tatami which would allow for the placement of an imaginary regular-size natsume between it and the tatami bordering material (*heri*). The chashaku is set out to the "lower" (*geza*) side of the natsume, so that its center is aligned with the center of the natsume.

Examining the Chasen, Folding the Chakin, and Wiping the Chawan

The importance placed on cleanliness in chanoyu is highlighted in the following passage from Rikyū's poems on the Way of Tea (*Rikyū dōka*): "Things that are best if they are fresh are the cold water, hot water, chakin, chasen, chopsticks and yōji, hishaku, and one's heart." When you are having guests, in particular the chasen and chakin which you use should be brand-new.

The temae technique for checking the tines of and purifying the chasen is called *chasentōshi*. During a temae, the host does this before whisking the tea as well as when the temae is being brought to a close. Of course, before the temae even begins, the chasen should be carefully pre-checked in the mizuya during the preparations, to make sure the tines are perfectly clean and none are broken.

The chakin is used to wipe the chawan following the examining of the chasen, as well as for other purposes. The chakin preparations in the mizuya involve soaking the chakin in water, wringing it out tightly, folding it, and placing it in the chawan. This generally is a part of the preparation work done in the mizuya, but on occasion the chakin is wrung and folded in the tea room in view of the guests.

Examining the chasen

During a temae, before the chasen is put to use to prepare the tea, the tines are passed through the hot water and are also thoroughly checked, in the technique called *chasentōshi*. When the temae is being brought to a close, a simpler inspection of the chasen tines is conducted, which is also called *chasentōshi*. The following directions are for the former, main instance of *chasentōshi*.

After putting hot water in the chawan, pick up the chasen with your right hand, set it into the chawan, and as the thumb and forefinger keep hold of the chasen handle, straighten the other three fingers and rest the middle finger on the chawan rim while setting the chasen handle down and releasing the thumb and forefinger. Simultaneously, stabilize the chawan at the left with your left hand.

Regrasp the chasen so that your right thumb is over the handle.

Raise the chasen and bring it to a horizontal angle. Then, as you rotate your wrist inward, return the chasen to the chawan.

Set the chasen into the chawan as in step 1. Repeat steps 2–3.

Regrasp the chasen.

Raise the chasen.

Rest the chasen in the chawan for the third time. Regrasp the chasen for use.

Lightly whisk the chasen back and forth through the hot water in the chawan in an act of purification.

Draw a circle in the style of the hiragana character "の". Toward the end, straighten your left fingers and bring the hand to face up in touching the chawan. While slowly removing the chasen from the chawan, place your left hand at rest on your left thigh.

How to fold the chakin

The mizuya should be equipped with a shallow tub (chakindarai) for soaking and rinsing the chakin. Place the diagonally opposite corners of the soaking chakin together and temporarily hang these "ears" over the rim of the tub. With your right thumb and forefinger, lift the dripping chakin out of the tub. With your left hand, grasp the chakin around the middle and, while lowering the right hand that holds the two "ears," bend the lower portion up and under, allowing the righthand "ears" to protrude from the right. Regrasp the chakin with both hands and wring out the excess moisture. Then fold the chakin as follows, continually taking care to align the edges and, from steps 3 to 10, to keep the chakin taut.

Take the protruding ears, one with your right hand and the other with your left.

Fold the top third down and away from you.

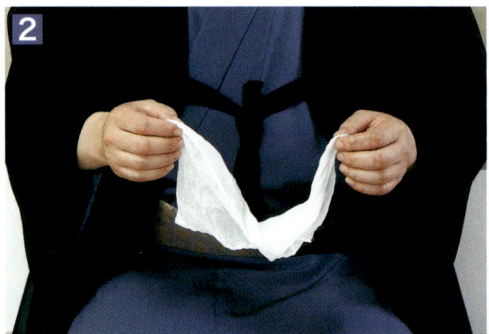

Pull them apart.

Fold down again, so that the chakin is evenly folded into thirds.

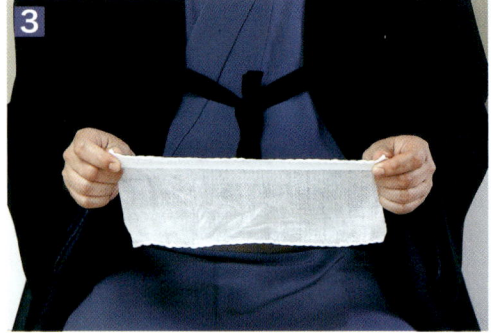

Rehold the chakin, making sure that the stitched hem along the top is on the side facing you, and pull the chakin taut.

Face your right palm down while moving the arm so that the chakin is vertical over your left thigh and arm is horizontal. Clasp the chakin at the middle between your left thumb and fingers.

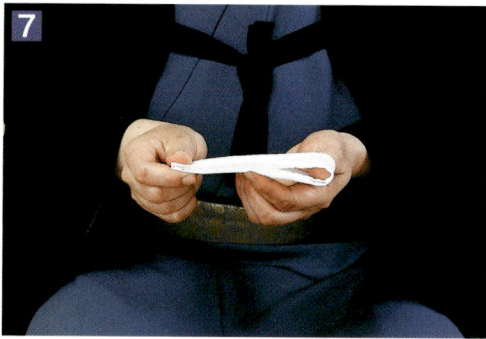

Move your right hand down and left hand up, folding the chakin in half lengthwise, where your left thumb remains, and regrasp both of the righthand edges with your right hand as you bring the chakin horizontally in front of your body.

Press you left fingertips into the chakin from underneath, at the halfway point, and fold the righthand portion of the chakin down against those fingertips.

Hold the new righthand fold with your right thumb and fingers, while bringing the left fingers under the chakin which is now folded into fourths lengthwise.

Press your left fingertips into the chakin from underneath at the two-thirds point, fold the righthand portion of the chakin under against the left fingers, and rehold that portion with your right hand. Adjust your pull to bring the chakin into neat order.

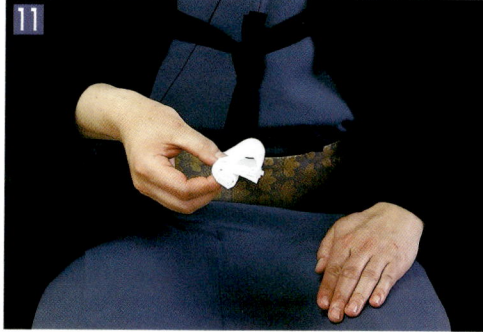

Keeping hold of the chakin with your right hand, carefully take your left thumb out so that the hollow left by it stays nicely puffed, and bring your left hand to rest on your left thigh. (Side note: The puff is called "*fukudame,*" or "place for accumulating good fortune.")

Set the chakin inside the chawan so that the puff is closest to the front.

How to wipe the chawan

After hot water is poured into the chawan and that water is emptied into the kensui (waste-water receptacle), the chawan needs to be wiped. The chakin is used for this, as described here.

You have set the chakin inside the chawan, putting its puff closest to the front. Hold the portion having the puff with your right thumb and forefinger and lift upward as shown.

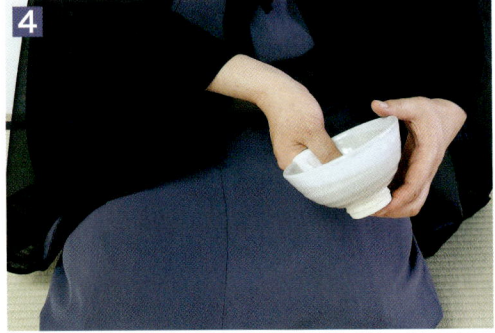

Slide the chakin around clockwise to where your left hand holds the chawan, grip the chawan through the chakin, loosen your left hand hold, turn the chawan counterclockwise to bring your right hand to its step 3 position, and tighten your left hand hold again. Repeat this two more times.

As you hold the chawan over your left knee with your left hand, rotate your right hand outward so that the thumb is above, and drape that half of the chakin over the left edge of the chawan just above where your left hand holds it.

Slide the chakin around halfway, and as you make sure that the chawan front faces you, bring the chawan so that it is directly in front of you.

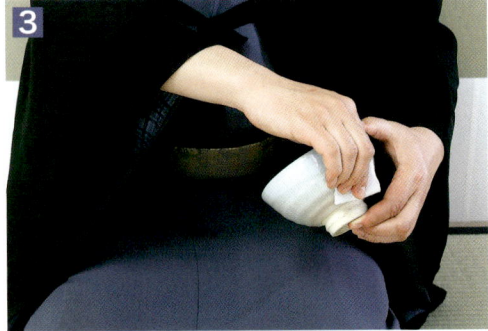

Clasp the chakin that is draped over the chawan between your right thumb, which is within the chawan, and forefinger, pressing from the exterior. The other three fingers should be aligned with the forefinger.

Pull the chakin off of the chawan.

Rotate your hand inward, and with your right thumb above and four fingers below, lay the chakin inside the chawan.

Continuing that move, fold the far portion of the chakin inward one third.

Rotate your right hand outward this time so that the one-third portion can be held between the forefinger from above and thumb from the back side.

Rotate your right hand so that the palm faces down, and swab the chawan interior first as though writing the hiragana character "い" and then the narrower hiragana character "り" to wipe the center of the chawan's interior.

Set the chakin inside the chawan so that it is just as when you started at step 1 herein, with its puff closest to the front.

Rehold the chawan with your right hand and set it down in front of you.

Handling the Hishaku

As mentioned earlier, cleanliness is of paramount concern in chanoyu. Like the chakin and chasen, a pristine hishaku should always be readied. There are three main types of hishaku: 1) the type for use when a furo (brazier) is being used for the temae; 2) the type for use when a ro (sunken hearth) is being used for the temae; and 3) the type for use for temae in which the hishaku is on display in the tea room. This third kind is called *sashitōshi* in reference to the fact that the handle (*e*) "pierces through" the cup (*gō*). With the first two types, the end of the handle which fits onto the cup is shaped to fit the curvature of the cup and is called *tsukigata*, for its resemblance to a crescent moon. The bottom tip of the handle is called the *kiridome*, or "cut end." The *kiridome* of the three hishaku types are characterized as follows: *sashitōshi*, straight-cut; furo-use hishaku, slanted inward from front to back side of the handle; ro-use hishaku, slanted outward from front to back side.

During a temae, there are the following especially notable manners in which the hishaku is handled:

Kagami-bishaku

This refers to a certain pose taken when using the hishaku; it is the "mirror ladle" pose. The main occasion for it is when the hishaku is first taken in hand during the temae; that is, when you take the hishaku from the top of the kensui. To do this, take it with your left hand and, while rotating that hand inward, bring the hishaku vertically in front of you. Lightly hold the bottom of the handle with your right hand, and tilt the hishaku so that the cup faces you straight forward while also repositioning your left thumb and forefinger to firmly hold the handle just below the node. Straighten your right hand fingers, keeping the fingertips just touching the handle end. This is the *kagami-bishaku* pose.

Oki-bishaku, kiri-bishaku, hiki-bishaku

When a furo is being used for the temae, there are three distinctive manners in which the hishaku is set on the kettle. That called *oki-bishaku* is done in such cases as before the initial examining of the chasen or when rinsing out a used chawan; that called *kiri-bishaku* is done after pouring the excess hot water back into the kettle after ladling hot water into the chawan for the making of the tea; and that called *hiki-bishaku* is done after ladling cold water.

Kagami-bishaku

Hishaku use with furo temae

Oki-bishaku

This is how to rest the hishaku on the kettle after you have poured hot water from the hishaku into the chawan, such as before the initial examining of the chasen (*chasentōshi*) or when rinsing out a used chawan.

Extend your arm at a natural angle and rest the hishaku cup level on the far side of the mouth of the kettle.

Draw your thumb out from underneath and lightly hold the hishaku just below the node with your thumb on top and forefinger underneath.

Lower the hishaku handle so that it rests on the near side of the mouth of the kettle, at the kettle's front center point.

Kiri-bishaku

This is how to rest the hishaku on the kettle after ladling hot water into the chawan to make the tea and pouring the excess hot water back into the kettle.

Extend your arm at a natural angle, and rest the hishaku cup level on the far side of the mouth of the kettle.

Without changing the position of the hishaku, extend your thumb to the left and fingers upward so that the hishaku handle rests where the thumb and fingers almost form a right angle.

Lower the hishaku handle so that it rests on the near side of the mouth of the kettle, at the kettle's front center point.

Hiki-bishaku

This is how to rest the hishaku on the kettle after ladling cold water.

Extend your arm at a natural angle, rest the hishaku cup level on the far side of the mouth of the kettle, then pull your hand slightly back from the node.

Arch the thumb back and toward yourself, and circle it around the bottom tip of the handle.

Continuing that move, bring the thumb together with the other fingers.

With the hishaku handle still resting along the tips of your right fore- and middle fingers, pull your hand to the bottom end of the hishaku handle.

During the previous steps, also bring the hishaku into alignment with the front center of the kettle.

Curl your fingers as though forming a ring with your thumb and fingers, and carefully lower the hishaku handle.

Rest the hishaku handle on the mouth of the kettle, at the kettle's front center point.

Drawing hot water from the kettle

This is how to handle the hishaku in order to draw hot water from the kettle which is resting above the fire in the furo.

With your right hand thumb and fingers aligned, lift up the bottom tip of the hishaku handle.

The handle naturally comes to lie between the thumb and extended forefinger and rest on the side of the slightly curved middle finger. Stop and grasp the hishaku firmly when your forefinger reaches the node.

Slide your hand toward the node while rotating the hand so your palm faces leftward and while also raising the handle until the hishaku cup is level. The line of the hishaku naturally angles outward as if it is an extension of the line made by your extended arm.

Scoop the hot water.

Taking the hishaku in order to draw water from the water jar

This is the furo temae version of the *tori-bishaku* technique used to take the hishaku which is resting on the kettle and rehold it in order to draw cold water.

With your right hand thumb and forefinger, grasp the hishaku handle from above and raise the handle until the hishaku cup is level.

Slide your right fingers to the end of the handle.

Remove the hishaku from the kettle and bring it horizontally over your knees.

Swivel your right hand to hold the handle from underneath, with it lying between the thumb and extended forefinger and resting on the side of the slightly curved middle finger.

Grasp the handle at the node with your left thumb above and forefinger underneath.

Slide your right hand toward the node. Stop and grasp the hishaku firmly when your forefinger reaches the node, release your left hand, and scoop the water.

Hishaku use with ro temae

Resting the hishaku on the kettle
This is the ro temae method for resting the hishaku on the kettle.

Hang the cup of the hishaku face downward just within the mouth of the kettle. As you lower the tip of the handle to the tatami, clasp the handle between your forefinger and middle finger, then release your right thumb from the handle and move it out from under the handle to align with your forefinger.

Drawing hot water from the kettle
This is how to take the hishaku which is resting on the kettle and draw hot water from the kettle.

With the forefinger and middle finger of your right hand, clasp the hishaku handle at a point slightly lower than the node.

While raising the handle with your forefinger and middle finger, bring the thumb underneath and around the handle, then grasp the handle firmly and, as you rotate your hand to the right, dip the hishaku cup into the hot water.

Draw up the hot water.

Taking the hishaku in order to draw water from the water jar

This is the ro temae version of the *tori-bishaku* technique used to take the hishaku which is resting on the kettle and rehold it in order to draw cold water.

Grasp the hishaku handle from above with your right thumb and forefinger, at a point somewhat lower than the node.

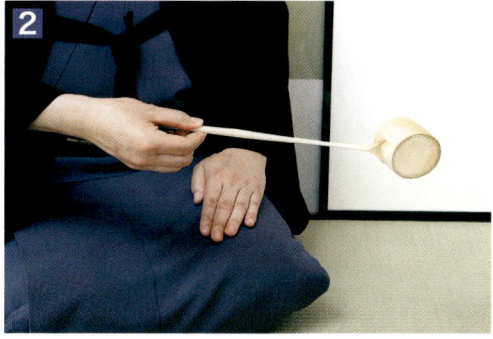

Remove the hishaku from the kettle and, as you rotate your hand inward to turn the hishaku cup upward, bring the hishaku over your knees.

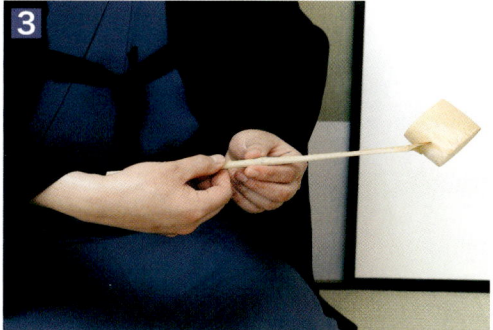

Grasp the handle at a point just lower than the node with your left thumb and forefinger, and continue to turn the hishaku until it is straight across your knees with the scoop facing upward.

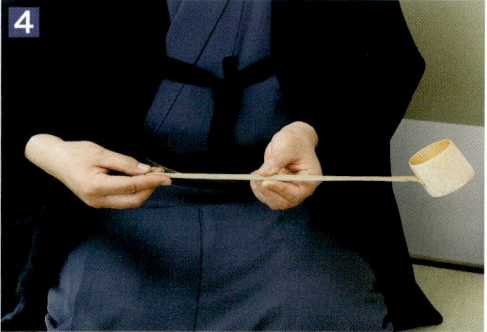

Slide your right fingers to the bottom tip of the handle.

Swivel your right hand to hold the handle from underneath, with it lying between the thumb and extended forefinger and resting on the side of the slightly curved middle finger, then slide your hand like that up, stopping and grasping the hishaku firmly when your forefinger is about 1.5 cm from the node.

Release your left hand, and scoop the water.

Preparations in the Mizuya

The preparation room connected to the tea room is known as the *mizuya*. What we call "mizuya preparation," however, is not limited to the preparation work that we do in that room; it refers to all the preparations, including those of the tea room. If your preparations are insufficient, you can not very well receive guests. However, the things for a host to keep in mind concerning the mizuya preparation when welcoming guests can not be mastered in a day. You gradually master them by working hard at your study session preparations, approaching each regular study session as if it were an actual tea gathering.

In the mizuya, cleanliness is top priority, with necessary implements orderly arranged for ease of use. Movements should be swift and quiet, sensible, and with attention to detail.

First of all, wash your hands, and then wash and fold the chakin with your cleansed hands, as learned during your practice of the temae fundamentals. A new chakin will have been starched and needs thorough washing to eliminate the starch in order to make it useable. After usage, also, a chakin requires thorough washing. Once washed, it is temporarily kept in the chakindarai (the shallow tub that is meant for this) with its two "ears" hanging over the rim of the chakindarai.

Before the chasen is arranged in the chawan, its tines must be lightly run through water. Confirm the front of the chawan, and also make sure that the knot of the chasen's woven thread faces upward. Some new chasen arrive with the foot pasted to the box, and therefore have dried paste adhering to their foot. First loosen the paste by wetting the foot in the chakindarai, and then wipe off the paste with a cloth.

In the case of a futaoki (lid rest) that is made of bamboo, rinse it with water and lightly wipe it dry with a towel. If the futaoki has a *kaō* (stylized monogram signature) on it, take extra care. As for the hishaku, rinse all of it, from cup to handle end, with water and then remove the excess moisture with a towel. The kensui (waste-water receptacle) tends to be handled carelessly by many people, but like any other article in chanoyu, it should not be dragged across the floor, whether the floor is wooden or tatami and no matter what kind of kensui it is. Laying the kensui upside down on the sunoko (bamboo drainboard that is over the sink in the mizuya) can damage the mouth of the kensui, so take care when doing this.

A kashiki (confection container) which has been retrieved from the tea room needs to be refreshed if it is going to be used further. The confections must be reset, and if kuromoji chopsticks go with the kashiki, they must be wetted and placed across the kashiki, making sure that they are going across the front side.

The implements which you use in your temae, you are to clean up and return to their proper place. It may be that someone else did the preparation of the implements for you; nonetheless, as the one to do temae with them, the final responsibility for their preparation is yours, and so you should take a moment to personally verify the implements before use and after cleanup, no matter the situation.

Bonryaku Temae

About the Bonryaku Temae

The Bonryaku temae (Bonryaku-demae) was designed by Ennōsai, the 13th generation Urasenke iemoto, and like the *ryūrei-shiki* temae which is done sitting on a chair as opposed to on tatami, it is among the temae which originated at Urasenke. It is considered a good procedural sequence to begin with when learning how to actually make a bowl of tea once you have mastered the temae basics. The standard hot-water equipment for this temae consists in a binkake (small brazier for heating a teapot) and tetsubin (cast iron teapot). The following guide to the temae is based on the premise that these are being used. It is possible to substitute the binkake and tetsubin with a typical hot-water kettle or thermos with handle and spout, in which cases the temae procedures will change accordingly. This flexibility makes this temae, as well as the Chitose-bon temae (pages 87-116) which is based on it, well-suited for enjoying chanoyu casually in the family room or study at your home, at your business office, and so on.

The Preparations

In the tea room: In the right-left center of the upper half of the temaedatami (the tatami on which, in its upper half, the temae equipment is arranged), place the binkake on a board (*shikiita*) that is of the appropriate size, set a trivet inside, and set the tetsubin on the trivet. Once the water in the tetsubin has become piping hot, adjust the lid so that the mouth is open a crack at the back. In the mizuya: Arrange the chawan (with the chakin and chasen inside, and chashaku resting face down across the right) and natsume on a tray approximately 30 centimeters in diameter which has a standing rim that is not excessively high. (The tray shown is a Yamamichibon, named for its undulating rim that resembles an undulating mountain path). Have a kensui out and ready, as well.

Carrying out the tea implements

Sit at the sadōguchi (host's doorway connecting the tea room and mizuya) with the tray that holds the chawan and natsume placed to the wall post side. Open the fusuma (1), and make a *shin* bow (2). Using both hands, pick up the tray. Enter the room with your right foot (3), proceed to the temaeza (4), sit, and place the tray directly in front of the binkake (5).

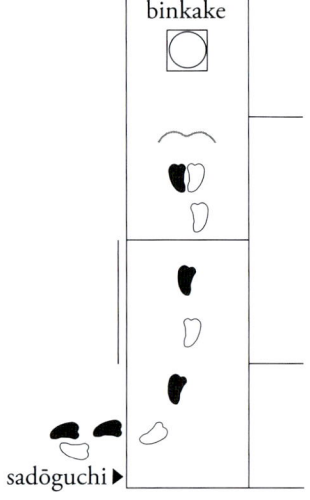

Leading with your left foot, stand, turn, and return to the mizuya. Hold the kensui at your side with your left hand, and return to the tea room (6). Sit directly in front of the tray (7), and set down the kensui (8). Pick up the tray, hold it just above knee level (9), adjust your sitting position to face diagonally toward the guest side (10), and set the tray down. Hold the kensui with your left hand and move it forward so that it is halfway inside the upper half of the temaedatami (11). Make sure your clothing is not in disarray, and pause in the proper sitting position for a moment of concentration (12).

Purifying the natsume

Take your fukusa from your obi with your left hand (13), and fold it for purifying the natsume (14). See "Folding the fukusa," pages 37-39.

Pick up the natsume from its side with your left hand (15), and purify it. See "Purifying the natsume," pages 40-41. Wipe the lid's far and near surfaces (16). Let the fukusa spread open on top of the lid and place your open palm on top (17). Push the hand forward slightly, then, moving from the elbow, let the hand slide off the lid to the right (18). Remember to let the hand slide outward and not drop too soon, as though you were wiping a second lid next to the first. For this temae, place the natsume down on the far side of the tray, to the left of center (19).

Purifying the chashaku

Refold the fukusa (20), and rest it on your left palm (21). Take the chashaku with your right hand (22), set it on the fukusa, scoop facing upward (23), and purify it by wiping with the fukusa three times. See "Purifying the chashaku," pages 44-45. The first wipe is to purify the top and bottom surfaces (24).

The next wipe is to purify the sides (25), and the third wipe once again purifies the top and bottom surfaces (26). Slide the fukusa forward and off from the tip of the chashaku (27). Bring your left hand lightly to rest on your left thigh.

Place the chashaku somewhat diagonally on the near side of the tray to the right of center, resting its handle on the rim of the tray (28). Move your right hand directly to the handle of the chasen, take it with the thumb and forefinger (29), draw the chasen out of the chawan, and stand it on the far side of the tray, to the right of center, so it forms a balanced pair with the natsume (30). Take the chakin from the chawan and place it directly to the right on the tray (31).

Pouring hot water into the chawan

Transfer the fukusa to your right hand by placing the right thumb into the folded-over fukusa and right fingers under that right side. Place the fukusa on the tetsubin lid and utilize it to grasp the knob and close the lid (32). Bring your right hand back, still holding the fukusa as before, and bring it lightly to rest on your right thigh. Grasp the tetsubin handle with your left hand (33). Flip your right hand, which holds the fukusa, over and utilize the fukusa to secure the tetsubin lid as you pour hot water into the chawan (34).

Return the tetsubin to the binkake, and, with your right hand, place the fukusa left of center on the tray, with its left side resting on the rim (35). The implements on the tray should appear like this at this point (36).

Examining the chasen

Take the chasen with your right hand and proceed with *chasentōshi*, the examining of the chasen. See "Examining the chasen," pages 46-47. After placing the chasen in the chawan, raise it to a horizontal angle and check the tines (37). Repeat this process. In the end, whisk the tines back and forth through the hot water, move the chasen in a circular motion as though drawing the hiragana character "の", and lift the chasen out of the bowl (38).

Return the chasen to where it was on the tray (39). Take the chawan with your right hand (40), transfer it to your left hand (41), and pour the water out into the kensui (42). Take the chakin with your right hand and place it inside the chawan (43).

Wiping the chawan

Hang the chakin over the left edge of the chawan (44). See "How to wipe the chawan," pages 50-51. Wipe the chawan by rotating the chakin around it about three-and-a-half times (45). Wipe the inside as if writing the hiragana characters "い" and "り" (46). Set the chakin in the chawan, rehold the chawan with your right hand, and return the chawan to where it was on the tray (47). Place the chakin back where it was on the tray (48).

Making and serving the usucha

Take the chashaku with your right hand. Invite the guests to go ahead and eat the confection (49) ("Okashi o dōzo"). Take the natsume with your left hand and bring it to the left of the chawan. Grasp the chashaku in your right palm using your ring finger and little finger, and remove the lid of the natsume with your thumb, forefinger, and middle finger (50). Rest the lid on the rim of the tray where the chashaku was resting (51). Hold the chashaku for use and put two scoops of tea into the chawan (52). Give the chashaku a light tap against the rim of the chawan to remove the excess tea (53).

Grasp the chashaku in your palm as before, put the natsume lid back on, and return the natsume to where it was (54), followed by the chashaku (55). Pick up the fukusa from the right with your right hand, then grasp the tetsubin handle with your left hand and, as before, pour hot water into the chawan (56). Return the tetsubin and fukusa to their respective places (57).

Take the chasen and, as you stabilize the chawan with your left hand, whisk the usucha (58). Return the chasen (59). Pick up the chawan with your right hand, place it on your left palm (60), in two clockwise moves, turn the chawan so that the front faces away from yourself (61), set the chawan out for the guest (62), and then sit in the ready position (63).

Acknowledge the guests expression of thankfulness for the tea ("Otemae chōdai itashimasu") with a *sō* bow (64).

Once the guest has finished the tea and returned the chawan, take the chawan with your right hand (65), rest it on your left palm, and re-hold it directly from the side with your right hand (66). Return the chawan to the tray (67).

Pour hot water into the chawan (68) and then pour that hot water out into the kensui (69). If the guest asks you to conclude ("Dōzo oshimai o"), acknowledge that (70), then return the chawan to the tray (71). While making a *sō* bow (72), say that you will conclude the temae ("Oshimai itashimasu").

Concluding the temae

Pour hot water into the chawan (73). Take the chasen with your right hand, and proceed with the simple version of *chasentōshi*, in which the chasen is raised only once (74). Pour the hot water out (75), take the chakin with your right hand, and rest it inside the chawan (76).

Return the chawan with the chakin inside to the tray (77). Return the chasen to the chawan (78). Pick up the chashaku with your right hand, then take the kensui with your left hand (79) and move it back so that it is fully within the lower half of the temae-datami (80). Holding the chashaku deeply in your right palm again, pick up the fukusa (81) and refold it for purifying the chashaku (82).

Purify the chashaku (83), this time wiping with the fukusa only twice, and place it on the chawan, scoop facing downward (84). Move your right hand directly to the natsume (85), and return the natsume to its original position on the tray (86). Dust off the fukusa over the kensui (87). Use the fukusa to set the tetsubin lid slightly ajar as it was at the start (88). Return the fukusa to your obi (89). Pick up the tray with both hands (90), move to face the binkake straightforward, and set the tray down (91).

Hold the kensui with your left hand and, leading with your left leg, stand up (92). Move your left foot around behind your right foot and diagonally back to the right (93), to turn away from the guests. Bring your right foot over to the bottom end of the temaedatami, and cross into the next tatami with your left foot (94). Return the kensui to the mizuya, leaving the room with your left foot (95). Reenter the tea room, sit in front of the tray, pick it up with both hands, and stand up as before (96). This time, move your left foot diagonally back to the left (97), to turn in the direction of the guests (98), and go to the mizuya, again leaving the room with your left foot. Upon exiting, turn around to face the tea room, sit, and place the tray to the wall post side (99). Make a formal *shin* bow (100), and close the fusuma sliding door.

82 *Bonryaku Temae*

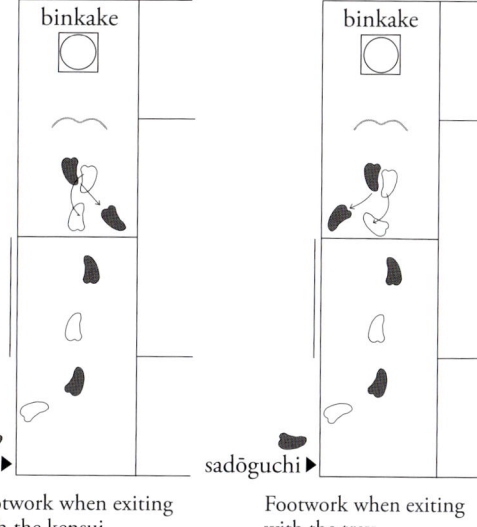

Footwork when exiting with the kensui

Footwork when exiting with the tray

Doing the Bonryaku Temae Facing the Binkake

Entering with the kensui at the start

It is possible to do the Bonryaku temae facing the binkake, as opposed to sitting diagonally toward the guest side. The procedure for this does not differ much from that described on pages 63-83. Here, only the differences in the temae will be introduced.

After entering with the kensui (page 64, step 6), proceed to the temaeza (1), sit directly in front of the tray, and set down the kensui so that the front edge of the kensui is flush with your knee line (2, 3). Make sure your clothing is not in disarray, and pause in the proper sitting position for a moment of concentration (4). After this, the temae steps are the same as page 65, step 13, through to page 78, step 78.

Returning to the mizuya at the end

After you have been asked to conclude the temae and you have thus finished the simple version of *chasentōshi,* returned the chawan to the tray, returned the chasen to its original position in the chawan, and now picked up the chashaku to purify it, leave the kensui as it is and immediately pick up the fukusa and refold it (1). From here, purify the chashaku (2), place it on the chawan, directly pick up the natsume and return it to its original position on the tray (3), and dust off the fukusa over the kensui (4), in the same manner described from page 78, step 81 through to page 80, step 89.

Use the fukusa to set the lid slightly ajar as it was at the start (5), then return the fukusa to your obi (6). Adjust your sitting position about about one knee's breadth diagonally toward the kensui, pick up the kensui with your left hand and, leading with your left foot, stand up (7). Return the kensui to the mizuya (8). Return to the tea room, remove the tray to the mizuya and, upon exiting, turn around to face the tea room, sit, and place the tray to the wall post side. Make a formal *shin* bow (9), and close the fusuma.

Chitose-bon Temae

About the Chitose-bon Temae

The Chitose-bon temae (Chitose-bon-demae) is the procedure for making tea when using the kind of large, round, lidded container called Chitose-bon created by Sen Kayoko (known posthumously as Seikō Myōka Taishi), wife of the 14th generation Urasenke iemoto, Mugensai, in commemoration of Mugensai's sixtieth birthday. Inside the lid of the original Chitose-bon, Kayoko inscribed a felicitous poem which includes the expression "chitose" ("a thousand years"). The lid of the Chitose-bon doubles as a tray when turned upside-down, and the Chitose-bon temae is a variant of the Bonryaku temae. Like the Bonryaku temae, it is very versatile, lending itself to most any kind of venue.

The Preparations

In the tea room: Arrange the binkake and tetsubin in the same manner as for the Bonryaku temae, placing them in the left-right center of the upper half of the temae-datami. Set the tetsubin lid ajar so that the tetsubin mouth is open a crack at the back. In the mizuya: Arrange the chawan (with the chakin and chasen inside, and chashaku resting face down across the right), natsume, and special small-sized kobukusa known as a *shiki-kobukusa* inside the Chitose-bon, as shown in the photo. The *shiki-kobukusa* has been folded in half, and its unsewn edge (*wasa*) should be up and to the right. Close the lid. Have a kensui out and ready, as well.

Carrying out the tea implements

Sit at the sadōguchi with the prepared Chitose-bon placed to the wall post side. Open the fusuma and make a *shin* bow (1). Pick up the Chitose-bon with both hands, stand up leading with your right foot, enter the room with your right foot, and head toward the temaeza (2). Cross into the temae-datami with your right foot (3), sit in front of the binkake (4), and set the Chitose-bon down (5). Then, leading with your left foot, stand, turn, and return to the mizuya. Hold the kensui at your side with your left hand, and return to the tea room (6). Sit in front of the Chitose-bon (7), and set down the kensui to your side (8). Make sure your clothing is not in disarray, and pause in the proper sitting position for a moment of concentration (9).

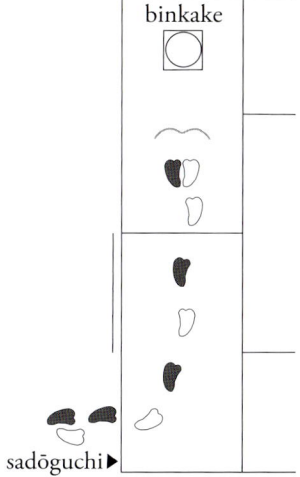

*Footwork when entering with the Chitose-bon

91

Purifying the Chitose-bon lid, natsume, and chashaku

Move the Chitose-bon to the left side of the tatami (10). Remove the lid with both hands (11). Bring the lid in front of you and turn the lid over left to right by bringing your left hand upward and lowering your right hand to hold the lid perpendicular. Change your right hand's hold on the lid, so that it is now just above your left hand's, then change your left hand's hold so that it is now where your right hand's was. Finish turning the lid over by bringing your hands level in front of you, and set the lid down in front of the binkake (12).

Remove your fukusa from your obi in the standard manner (13), and fold it as you would for purifying the natsume (14,15). See "Folding the fukusa," pages 37-39. In three strokes, as though drawing the character "三," purify the lid (16). Refold the fukusa in the same way (17). Take the natsume from the Chitose-bon with your left hand (18), and purify it (19). See "Purifying the natsume," pages 40-41.

Set the natsume on the far side of the Chitose-bon lid, to the left of center (20). Refold the fukusa for purifying the chashaku and rest it on your left palm (21). Pick up the chashaku with your right hand, and purify it (22). See "Purifying the chashaku," pages 44-45. Place the chashaku somewhat diagonally on the Chitose-bon lid to the right of center, resting its handle on the rim (23). Hold the bottom right-hand fold of the fukusa with your right hand, then hold the left-hand fold with your left hand, and set the fukusa down to the left, between the Chitose-bon and the kensui (24).

Pouring hot water into the chawan and examining the chasen

With your left hand, remove the *shiki-kobuku-sa* from the Chitose-bon (25). Transfer it to your right hand, which holds it at the fold, place it on the Chitose-bon lid, and open it out like opening a book from left to right (26). With both hands, remove the chawan from the Chitose-bon (27), and set it on the *shiki-kobukusa* (28).

Remove the chasen from the chawan (29), and stand it to the right of the natsume (30). Take the chakin from the chawan and place it directly to the right on the Chitose-bon lid (31). The arrangement of the implements on the Chitose-bon lid should appear like this at this point (32).

Pick up the fukusa with your left hand (33), transfer it to your right hand, and use it to close the tetsubin lid (34). Next, grasp the tetsubin handle with your left hand (35) and, securing the tetsubin lid with the fukusa in your right hand, pour hot water into the chawan (36). Return the tetsubin to the binkake, transfer the fukusa to your left hand, and return the fukusa to its former resting place (37).

Take the chasen with your right hand and proceed with *chasentōshi*, the examining of the chasen (38). See "Examining the chasen," pages 46-47. Return the chasen to where it was on the Chitose-bon lid and, continuing with that move, pick up the chawan with your right hand (39), transfer it to your left hand, and pour the water out into the kensui (40). Take the chakin with your right hand and use it to wipe the chawan in the standard manner (41). See "How to wipe the chawan," pages 50-51. Rehold the chawan with your right hand, set it back on the *shiki-kobukusa* (42), and return the chakin to its former place on the Chitose-bon lid.

Making and serving the usucha

Holding the chashaku in your right hand, invite the guests to go ahead and eat the confection ("Okashi o dōzo") (43). Take the natsume from the side with your left hand, secure the chashaku deep in your right palm with the last two fingers, use your right thumb and first two fingers to remove the natsume lid, and rest the lid where the chashaku was (44). Put two scoops of tea into the chawan (45). Give the chashaku a light tap against the rim of the chawan to remove the excess tea, replace the natsume lid, return the natsume to its former place (46), then return the chashaku to its former place.

Pick up the fukusa with your left hand (47), and transfer it to your right hand. Pour hot water into the chawan, using the fukusa to secure the tetsubin lid as before (48). Return the tetsubin to the binkake, transfer the fukusa to your left hand, and return the fukusa to its former resting place as before. Take the chasen and whisk the usucha (49). Pick up the chawan, turn it to face away from yourself, and set it out for the guest (50).

Acknowledge the guest's expression of thankfulness for the tea ("Otemae chōdai itashimasu") with a *sō* bow (51). Once the chawan is returned to you, take it with your right hand, rest it on your left palm, re-hold it from the side with your right hand, and set it down on the *shiki-kobukusa* (52). Pour hot water into the chawan (53), and empty that hot water into the kensui (54). If the guest asks you to bring the temae to a close ("Dōzo oshimai o"), acknowledge that (55). Set the chawan back down on the *shiki-kobukusa*. Make a *sō* bow as you tell the guest that you will bring the temae to a close ("Oshimai itashimasu") (56).

Concluding the temae

Pour hot water into the chawan (57). Conduct the simple version of *chasentōshi* (58). Pour the hot water out into the kensui (59). Take the chakin, and use it to wipe the chawan in the standard manner (60). Set the chawan with the chakin inside back on the *shiki-kobukusa* (61). Place the chasen in its original position in the chawan (62). Pick up the chawan with both hands (63), and return it to its original position in the Chitose-bon (64). Fold the *shiki-kobukusa* in half from right to left (65), pick it up with your right hand from the right side, transfer it to your left hand (66), and return it to its original position in the Chitose-bon (67).

103

Pick up the chashaku with your right hand (68). Take the fukusa with your left hand, grasping from its right side with your thumb underneath (69). Turn your wrist so that your palm is turned upward as you bring the fukusa in front of you. Holding the chashaku deeply in you right palm, take the upper right "ear" of the fukusa with your right thumb and forefinger (70), and refold the fukusa (71).

Purify the chashaku, wiping with the fukusa only twice (72), and place it on the chawan inside the Chitose-bon, scoop facing downward (73). With your right hand, pick up the natsume and place it in the center of the Chitose-bon lid (74). Dust off the fukusa over the kensui (75). With your right hand, use the fukusa to set the tetsubin lid slightly ajar as it was at the start (76). Return the fukusa to your obi (77).

This is the point when the guest might ask to do *haiken* of the natsume and chashaku. The temae process differs depending upon whether there will be *haiken* or not. If there *is* a request for *haiken*, continue as described in steps 78-112. If there is *no* request for *haiken*, follow the steps described on pages 114-116.

105

Setting out the implements for *haiken*

The guest has requested *haiken* of the natsume and chashaku. Acknowledge that with a *sō* bow (78). Take the Chitose-bon lid with both hands, hold it just above knee level, adjust your sitting position to face diagonally toward the guest side, and set the lid down (79). Remove your fukusa from your obi, and fold it for purifying the natsume (80). Pick up the natsume from its side with your left hand (81), and wipe the lid (82). Secure the clutched fukusa deep in your right palm with the last two fingers. Use your right thumb and first two fingers to remove the natsume lid, turn your right hand to check the underside of the lid (83), then place it on the center of the Chitose-bon lid (84, 85). Wipe the far and near edges of the natsume rim with two left to right motions, replace the lid of the natsume, and place it on the Chitose-bon lid to the right of center (86). Return the fukusa to your obi (87).

Move to face the binkake straightforward (88), take the chashaku with your right hand (89), transfer it to your left hand, move back to the diagonal angle facing the guest side (90), and place the chashaku on the Chitose-bon lid slightly left of center facing upward (91). Turn the Chitose-bon lid to face away from yourself by taking hold of the lid from the right and left (92), then repositioning your right hand to the far side and your left hand to the near side (93), lifting the lid slightly, and rotating it clockwise 90 degrees (94), setting it down once, and then repeating the re-holding and rotating process. Pick up the lid with both hands and set it out for the guests (95).

Guests' *haiken*

Once the host has left the room after having set out the items for *haiken*, it is the role of the first guest to go after the haiken items. As first guest, transport the Chitose-bon lid with natsume and chashaku on it to your seat, and place it in front of you outside the tatami bordering (*heri-soto*). The manner for viewing the implements is as follows: First excuse yourself to the next guest (*gyō* bow), then place your hands as in the *shin* bow position and view the implements in their entirety. Then take out your kobukusa, place it to the right of the Chitose-bon lid, and spread it open. Examine the natsume, and then place it on the kobukusa. Do the same with the chashaku. View the features of the Chitose-bon lid. Return the natsume and chashaku to the Chitose-bon lid, put away your kobukusa, and take a last look at all the implements. Pass the lid and implements to the next guest.

Leaving the room

Adjust your sitting position to face diagonally toward the kensui (96), pick up the kensui with your left hand, and, leading with your left leg, stand up (97). Move your left foot around behind your right foot and diagonally back to the right, to turn away from the guests. Bring your right foot over to the bottom end of the temaedatami, and cross into the next tatami with your left foot (98). (See footwork diagram, page 83) Return the kensui to the mizuya.

Come to the sadōguchi. Before reentering the tea room, note whether the haiken items have been returned and, if they have not, sit at the sadōguchi (99). Once the guests are settled after returning the haiken items, reenter the room from your right foot, return to the temaedatami, and sit directly facing the items. Answer any questions about the items (100). Holding the Chitose-bon lid with both hands (101), move to face the binkake, and set the lid down (102). Take the chashaku with your right hand and place it in its original position on the chawan inside the Chitose-bon (103). Take the natsume with your right hand, rest it on your left palm, regrasp it from above with your right hand, and place it in its original position inside the Chitose-bon (104, 105).

Pick up the lid with both hands (106), turn it over right to left this time (107), and replace it onto the Chitose-bon (108). Set the Chitose-bon in front of the binkake (109). Then firmly hold the Chitose-bon, stand leading with your left leg (110), turn in the direction of the guests, and exit to the mizuya (111). Upon exiting, turn around to face the tea room, sit, and place the Chitose-bon to the wall post side. Make a formal *shin* bow (112), and close the fusuma sliding door.

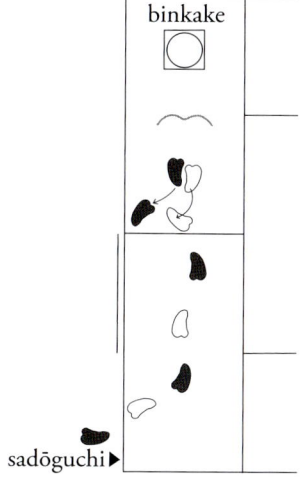

*Footwork when exiting with the Chitose-bon

Interesting variation

Instead of carrying the Chitose-bon into the tea room at the beginning of this temae (steps 1-5), you may start the temae with the Chitose-bon already displayed in front of the binkake. In that case, instead of having your fukusa tucked into your obi at the beginning, you can add a bit of flair to the arrangement by placing it on top of the Chitose-bon, folded as it would be to purify a chashaku. If you start the temae with the items displayed in this manner, it is appropriate to end it that way (after step 109) with the Chitose-bon displayed in front of the binkake and your fukusa placed on top.

When There Is No Request for *Haiken*

After concluding the temae (step 76, page 104) and returning your fukusa to your obi (1), if there is no request for *haiken*, do as follows: Pick up the natsume with your right hand (2), rest it on your left palm (3), re-grasp it from above with your right hand, and place it in its original position inside the Chitose-bon (4). Pick up the Chitose-bon lid with both hands (5), turn it over from right to left, and replace it onto the Chitose-bon (6). Set the Chitose-bon in front of the binkake (7). Adjust your sitting position to face diagonally toward the kensui (8).

Pick up the kensui with your left hand, and, leading with your left leg, stand up (9). Carry out the kensui (10). Hold the Chitose-bon with both hands, stand (11), and carry the Chitose-bon to the mizuya (12). Upon exiting the sadōguchi, turn around to face the tea room, sit, and place the Chitose-bon to the wall post side. Make a formal *shin* bow (13), and close the fusuma sliding door.

Knowledge for Guests

Entering the Tea Room

How to Partake of the Confections and Usucha

Entering the Tea Room

The guests' act of entering the tea room (*sekiiri*) involves a series of specific procedures, including first using the low stone water-basin called tsukubai which lies along the roji path leading to the tea room, next actually entering the room, then going up to the alcove to briefly take a respectful look at (*haiken*) the items there, furthermore going over to the tea-making area to briefly take a respectful look at the arrangements there, and finally taking their respective seats in the tea room.

The Tsukubai

The idea of conducting ablutions has long existed in Japan and is called *misogi* (purification ritual). Walking along the roji path, with each step the guests remove themselves from the secular world. Along the way, they stop at the tsukubai and rinse their hands and mouth, so as to be in a pure state to take part in the gathering which will unfold in the tea room.

The tsukubai area is composed of the following three functional stones besides the water-basin (*chōzubachi*) itself: a large, flat "front stone" on which to crouch to make use of the water-basin; on the right, a stone on which to place the portable candlestand (*teshoku*) used at gatherings held when it is dark outside; and on the left, a stone on which the host may rest the water pail (*teoke*). At extremely cold times of the year, the host might set a pail of warm water (*yuoke*) on that stone on the left, for use by the guests. The drain area between the water-basin and the "front stone," above which the actual rinsing of hands and mouth is conducted, is called *umi* (the sea).

Using the tsukubai

As you proceed along the roji path, you will come to the tsukubai. Tuck your fan into your obi, and crouch down on the front stone (1). Take the ladle with your right hand (2), scoop water (3), rinse your left hand using about half the water (4), then pass the hishaku to your left hand and rinse your right hand with the remaining water in the ladle (5).

Pass the ladle back to your right hand, scoop water one more time (6), pour some water into your left palm (7), and rinse your mouth with that (8). (Note: Never put your lips on the ladle.) Gently bring the ladle to a vertical angle to let the remaining water run over the handle, purifying it (9). Return the ladle to its original position on the water-basin (10). Use your handkerchief to wipe your hands and mouth, and then proceed to the tea room.

The interior of a small tea room

The interior of a spacious tea room

Tea Room Types

Having cleansed yourself of the dust of the everyday world as you made your way through the roji, you should reach the entrance of the tea room with mind free from thought or emotion and thus open to everything; the state of mind known as *mushin*. It is important to have an unaffected and pure attitude when you enter a tea room.

Depending upon the design of the tea room, its doorway for the guests may be of the small kind called nijiriguchi, which is unique to tea room architecture and was originally conceived by Sen Rikyū, or it may be a sliding shōji or fusuma. Commonly it will be a nijiriguchi if the tea room is 4.5 mats in size or smaller and the tea room thus falls into the "small room" (*koma*) category, whereas it will be a shōji or fusuma if the room is 4.5 mats in size or larger and thus falls into the "spacious room" (*hiroma*) category. A tea room that is exactly 4.5 mats in size is of the key size for a tea room and can be treated as either a small or a spacious room.

The names given to tatami mats based on their locations

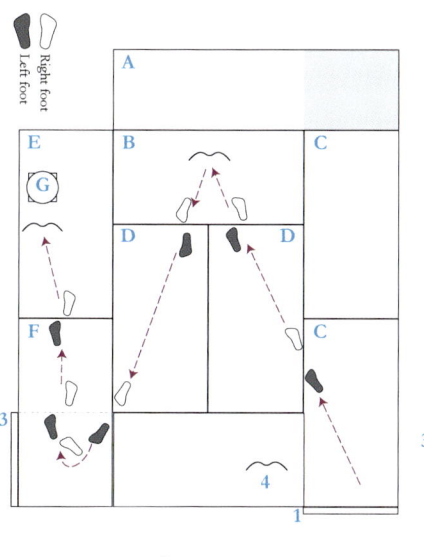

8 mat room

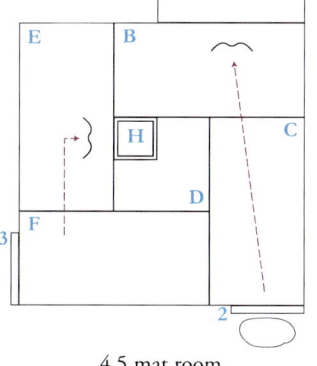

4.5 mat room

Tea room elements

- **A** Alcove / *Tokonoma*
- **B** High ranking personage's seating / *Kinindatami*
- **C** Guests' seating / *Kyakudatami*
- **D** Traversing mat / *Kayoidatami*
- **E** Temae mat / *Temaedatami* (Implement mat / *Dōgudatami*)
- **F** Host's entry mat / *Fumikomidatami*
- **G** Brazier / *Furo*
- **H** Sunken hearth / *Ro*

- **1** Spacious tea room guests' doorway (fusuma)
- **2** Small tea room guests' doorway (nijiriguchi)
- **3** Host's doorway / *Sadōguchi*
- **4** Temporary seating / *Kariza*

The nijiriguchi entrance to a small tea room

Entering Through a Nijiriguchi

The host will leave the nijiriguchi opened slightly, to let you, the guest, know you may enter from there and give you an initial handhold (*tegakari*). Crouch on the step-up stone which is in front of the nijiriguchi and place your right fingers in the nijiriguchi opening (1). Quietly slide the door panel until it is opened about halfway (2), then open it the rest of the way with your left hand (3).

Place your fan inside in front of you (4), place both hands on the floor, and survey the room (5). Moving your fan an arms length into the room and leaning forward while bracing yourself with your arms, enter head first (6) and, with legs in the seiza position, come fully into the room (7). With the help of your arms, swivel to face the nijiriguchi, moving first your fan and then your body (8), and in facing the nijiriguchi, place your fan to your right side (9).

Pick up your zōri which you took off and left on the step-up stone as you made your entry (10). Face the soles together (11) and place the zōri to the side, leaned against the zōri which are there already (12). If you are the last guest, whose responsibility it is to close and latch the door, then place your fan in front of you (13), close the door halfway with your right hand (14), and use your left hand to pull the door the rest of the way closed until the back of your hand touches the jamb of the door frame. Use your left hand to shut the door completely (15), allowing it to make a sound just loud enough that it can reach the ears of the host as a signal that all guests have entered the tea room. Close the door latch (16, 17).

Entering a Small Tea Room

(The example shown is a 4.5 mat tea room with sunken hearth in use, and with a scroll as well as flowers on display in the alcove.)

Upon entering the tea room, proceed to the alcove (1), place your fan in front of you, and make a *shin* bow to the scroll (2).

First take a respectful look at the scroll (3), and then the flowers and flower container (4). Finally, make another *shin* bow (5). Hold your fan in your right hand and, leading with your left leg, stand up (6). Stepping across the tatami borders/seams with your left foot, proceed to the half-mat that is adjacent to the host's doorway. Change direction and when proceeding to the temaedatami, lead with your right foot. Sit facing the hearth, place your fan in front of you, and take a respectful look at the kettle, the hearth frame, and so on (7).

Entering a Spacious Tea Room

Just as with a nijiriguchi, the shōji or fusuma panel will be opened slightly for the guests. Sit at the door, place your fan in front of you, and slide the door panel open (1). See "Opening and Closing Fusuma Siding Doors," pages 30-31. Place both hands on the floor and survey the room (2), set your fan an arms' length in front of you in the room, and slide into the room (3). Once inside, hold your fan in your right hand and, leading with your right leg, stand up (4). Stepping across the tatami borders with your right foot, proceed to the alcove (5).

Sit, place your fan in front of you, and make a *shin* bow to the scroll (6). First take a respectful look at the scroll (7), then the flowers and flower container (8), and finally make another *shin* bow. Hold your fan in your right hand and, leading with your left leg, stand up (9). Proceed to the half-mat that is directly in front of the host's doorway, stepping across the tatami borders with your left foot (10) and entering that half mat with your left foot (11). Change direction in that half-mat by taking two small steps, right foot, left foot, and then lead with your right foot in proceeding to the temaedatami (12). If there is only the brazier-kettle unit at the temaedatami, sit directly in front of it, place

your fan in front of you, and take a respectful look at the items, including the sculpted ash in the brazier and so on (13). If, besides the brazier-kettle unit there are other implements on display at the temaedatami, sit in the right-left center of the mat so that you can look at all of the items.

When there are multiple guests, they successively enter the tea room and proceed to the alcove around when the previous guest finishes viewing the alcove. After viewing the temaedatami arrangements, the first guest, whose seat is usually nearest to the alcove, finds a temporary sitting location (*kariza*), so as not to be in the way of the other guests as they go to view the alcove and the temaedatami. The other guests follow suit and take temporary seats next to the first guest. Set your fan next to your right knee when you are seated at a temporary sitting location (14).

If you are the last guest, it is your responsibility to close the door. Therefore, upon sliding into the room, swivel with the help of your arms to face the doorway, moving first your fan and then your body. Close the door in the standard manner, but in the final step, closing it against the jamb just firmly enough to make an audible sound, which serves to signal to the host that all guests have entered the tea room.

How to Partake of the Confections and Usucha

There are two types of prepared matcha: usucha (light, whisked matcha) and koicha (thick, blended matcha). This book will introduce how to partake of usucha and the confections which are commonly served with it.

About partaking of a bowl of usucha

In embarking upon chadō lessons, you are taught early on to express thankfulness for the confections and the tea and so on by raising them while making a slight bow before partaking of them. The practice of this at your lessons gradually cultivates a grateful heart towards all things, develops into a habit, and turns into something that you feel and do naturally. This spirit of thankfulness, this sense of gratitude, might also motivate you to take a moment to rethink your existence within the prosperous modern-day society in which you live. It is important to remember that, even though it may be within the context of a chadō lesson that you are partaking of a bowl of usucha, that act is an instantaneous opportunity to put the spirit and teachings of chadō into practice.

The confections served with matcha are basically of two types: omogashi (lit., main confection) and higashi (lit., dry confection). Conventionally, omogashi are served with koicha, and higashi are served with usucha. Sometimes, if the tea will be limited to usucha, omogashi rather than higashi will be offered, or on occasion, both may be offered.

The season finds expression in the flavor and the visual colors and shape of omogashi as well as higashi, and guests can sense how the host has put his heart into serving the confections by looking at their color combination and harmony with the containers they are served in or on. It would be a breach of etiquette and of the chadō spirit if a guest were not to eat the confection that the host served but to just take it home.

As first guest, make a *shin* bow in acknowledgment of the host's invitation to take the confections ("Okashi o dōzo").

Next make a *gyō* bow to the second guest, and excuse yourself for going ahead ("Osaki ni"). The second guest returns the bow.

Partaking of Higashi

The higashi which are served might be of just one type, two types, or several types. Starting with the first guest, the guests in turn will place one of each type on their kaishi and then pass the tray of higashi down. Before they take the higashi, they make a *gyō* bow to the next guest, saying, "Osaki ni," which means, "Excuse me for going before you." (This of course does not apply to the last guest.) They then, before taking the higashi, raise the tray slightly while simultaneously making a slight bow.

The last guest, after taking the higashi, returns the tray to the first guest (by either taking it or passing it back, depending upon the particular circumstances). The tray is returned because, after the first round of usucha, the guests may have additional helpings, in which case they may like to have more higashi as well and the tray will be passed down again.

Pick up the tray of higashi and raise it slightly in an expression of thankfulness.

Take out your kaishi and set it in front of you with the fold (*wasa*) toward you.

Lightly secure the tray with your left fingers as you take the higashi with your right fingers.

If there are two types of higashi, take the further one first, then the closer one.

Pass the tray to the second guest, keeping the tray outside the tatami bordering.

Pick up the kaishi and eat the higashi.

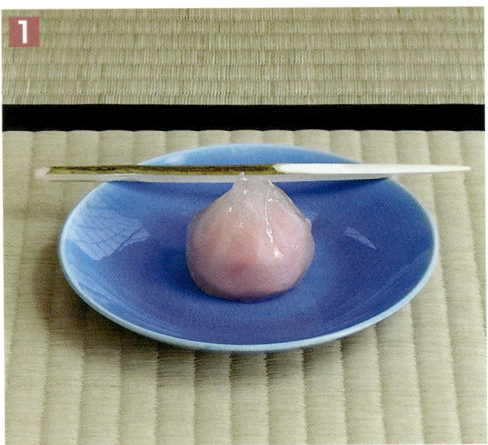

An omogashi which is served on an individual plate will conventionally be accompanied by a kuromoji sweets pick.

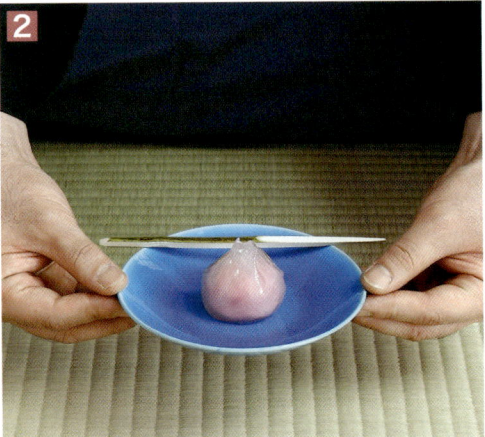

Pick up the plate with both hands and raise it slightly in an expression of thankfulness.

Take out your kaishi.

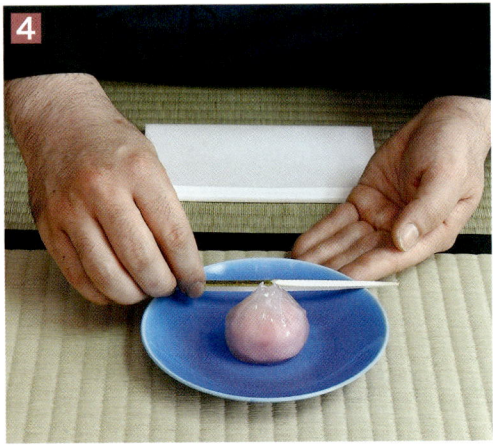

Take the kuromoji with your right hand while lightly securing the plate with the fingers of your left hand.

Place the omogashi on your kaishi. To eat it, pick up the kaishi and use the kuromoji.

Partaking of an Omogashi Which Is Individually Served

Omogashi are served one per guest. It might come to you on an individual plate (meimei-zara), or in a serving bowl (kashibachi) which holds enough for several guests. Even in the former case, the proper guest etiquette is to transfer the omogashi to your kaishi and eat it from that.

Pick up the container with both hands and raise it slightly in an expression of thankfulness. Then take out your kaishi.

Take the pair of kuromoji serving chopsticks with your right hand while lightly securing the container with the fingers of your left hand.

Place an omogashi on your kaishi.

Wipe the tips of the chopsticks using the corner of the top sheet of your kaishi.

Return the chopsticks to their original position across the front of the container, and then pass the container to the next guest, keeping it outside the tatami bordering.

Partaking of Omogashi Which Are Served in a Serving Bowl

When omogashi for several guests are served in a serving bowl or other such container, you take your piece onto your kaishi and then pass the container to the next guest.

Partaking of Usucha

As with partaking of confections, before drinking usucha the guests express thankfulness for it by raising the chawan somewhat while making a slight bow. Guests also avoid drinking from the chawan front. This is done by rotating the chawan before drinking.

Partaking of usucha alone or with other guests is one of the most fundamental things that you will do as a chadō student. Explained here is the etiquette for partaking of usucha when you are the only guest. The etiquette for multiple guests is explained in the next section (page 139).

Going to get your tea

When going to get the tea that has been prepared for you, the manner in which you should do so will depend upon whether you are in a spacious tea room (*hiroma*), or in a small tea room (*koma*). In a spacious tea room, you should walk and get it. For this, you stand up and move forward from your right foot, sit and pick up the chawan, and then stand up and return to your seat leading with your left foot.

In a small room, you remain in the seiza position and move forward or backward by pressing your hands to the floor to scoot yourself in the desired direction. When you are transporting the chawan (or any other item) in this way, you will likely need to repeat the process of taking it and placing it in front of you and moving a short distance until you reach your destination. Note that when returning to your seat in this manner, you back up without turning around.

After going to get your tea and returning to your seat, with your right hand, place the chawan in front of you inside the tatami bordering.

Make a *shin* bow to the host, and express thanks for the tea that you are about to drink ("Otemae chōdai itashimasu").

Pick up the chawan with your right hand and place it on your left palm.

Bow slightly while raising the chawan somewhat, in an expression of thankfulness.

Pick up and rotate the chawan about a quarter of a turn with your right hand.

Rotate the chawan once more. The chawan front no longer faces you.

Drink the tea.

With your right thumb and forefinger, wipe where your lips touched the chawan rim.

Rotate the chawan twice counter-clockwise with your right hand, returning the front to face you.

Place the chawan in front of you, this time outside the tatami bordering.

Place both hands as in the *shin* bow position, and view the chawan in its entirety.

Carefully take the chawan in both hands, and, without lifting it far from the floor, examine its details.

Set the chawan down outside the tatami bordering.

View the chawan in its entirety once more.

Place the chawan on your left palm, steady it with your right hand, and return it to the host.

The first guest has gotten the prepared tea and brought it back to his seat.

He places the chawan between himself and the next guest, inside the tatami bordering, makes a *gyō* bow, and excuses himself for going first ("Osaki ni").

Partaking of Usucha When There Are Multiple Guests

When multiple guests are served usucha in a single seating, they will get and partake of their individual serving in the order of their seating. The basic etiquette for partaking of it is explained on pages 136 to 138. The following explanation focuses on the interaction between guests.

If you are the first guest, upon fetching your usucha you place it between yourself and the next guest and excuse yourself for going ahead ("Osaki ni"). Then you place the chawan in front of you and express thanks to the host for the tea.

If you are seated between other guests, you acknowledge the guests to both sides before you thank the host for the tea and then drink it. First you offer your tea to the preceding guest, saying "Would you like another serving?" ("Mō ippuku ikaga desu ka"), and when that person declines, replying with "I will share in the hospitality" ("Oshōban itashimasu"). You then excuse yourself to the next guest, for going ahead of that person ("Osaki ni").

He places the chawan in front of himself inside the tatami bordering, makes a *shin* bow to the host, and expresses thanks for the tea ("Otemae chōdai itashimasu").

He places the chawan on his left palm, and bows slightly while raising the chawan somewhat, in an expression of thankfulness.

He drinks the usucha, having rotated the chawan to avoid drinking from the front.

The guest in the middle has gotten the prepared tea and brought it back to her seat.

She places the chawan between herself and the guest ahead of her, inside the tatami bordering.

She makes a *gyō* bow, offers her tea to that guest ("Mō ippuku ikaga desu ka?"), and when that guest declines, she replies that she will share in the hospitality ("Oshōban itashimasu").

She places the chawan between herself and the next guest, inside the tatami bordering.

She makes a *gyō* bow and excuses herself for going first ("Osaki ni").

She places the chawan in front of herself, inside the tatami bordering, makes a *shin* bow to the host, and expresses thanks for the tea ("Otemae chōdai itashimasu").

She places the chawan on her left palm, and bows slightly while raising the chawan somewhat, in an expression of thankfulness.

She drinks the usucha, having rotated the chawan to avoid drinking from the front.

In the case of the last guest, the steps are the same as for a middle guest (steps 6 to 13 above), except that there is no further guest, and therefore steps 9 and 10 do not apply.

Glossary

binkake 瓶掛
A small brazier in which a teapot, such as an iron tetsubin or silver ginbin, is placed on an iron trivet over a charcoal fire to heat hot water. Binkake are employed for the Bonryaku, Chitose-bon, and various chabako (portable, boxed set of implements for tea-making) temae.

chadō 茶道
Lit., "tea way"; the Way of Tea. Used as an alternative term for chanoyu, though the two terms carry different implications. Chadō, considered the formal term, emphasizes the philosophical spirit and aesthetic sensibilities which underscore the practice of chanoyu as a path of self-cultivation. "Sadō" is an alternate pronunciation of "chadō."

chadōgu 茶道具
Tea implement(s). The paraphernalia used for chanoyu, including but not limited to the temae implements (*temaedōgu*). For instance, hanging scrolls (kakemono) which are used in tea rooms are counted as tea implements.

chaji 茶事
A formal chanoyu function. Classically, there seven types, ranging from the representative full tea function (*shōgo*) to the spontaneous serving of tea for an unexpected guest. The *shōgo* function includes, among other things, the host's building of the charcoal fire as the guests watch, the serving of a kaiseki meal, and the serving of both koicha and usucha.

chakai 茶会
A tea get-together less lengthy than a chaji, at which the host generally serves omogashi to the guests and prepares only usucha, or not so commonly, only koicha. Oftentimes, chakai are held for a large number of guests, and several seatings (*seki*) are held in order to accommodate them.

chakin 茶巾
A bleached linen cloth of specified measurements used for wiping tea implements in the course of temae.

chakindarai 茶巾盥
The small tub used in the mizuya for soaking and rinsing the chakin. Most chakindarai are made of bronze or cast metal alloy. It is used on the slatted bamboo drainboard of the mizuya sink.

chanoyu 茶の湯
Lit., "hot water for tea." Used as an alternative term for chadō, though the two terms carry different implications. This is the popular, older and more general term. The art of enjoying matcha.

chaseki 茶席
The room or space where tea will be made and served; tea/chanoyu venue. It may or may not be a traditional style chashitsu.

chasen 茶筅
Tea whisk. It is made of a single length of bamboo and used to whisk/blend koicha and usucha.

chasentōshi 茶筅通し
Name of the temae technique involving the checking and purifying of the chasen.

chashaku 茶杓
Tea scoop. Most are made of a thin piece of bamboo, though there are some which are made of wood or other materials.

chashitsu 茶室
An architectural space designed for conducting chanoyu. The term may apply to a free-standing tea house or a tea room located within a larger building.

chawan 茶碗
Tea bowl. A bowl, most often ceramic, intended for the preparation and drinking of matcha.

fukusa 帛紗
Silk purifying cloth. It is double-layered, with one edge being formed of the fold (*wasa*), and the remaining three edges sewn together. It is the symbol of the host, and is worn whenever serving tea. Women use crimson or scarlet ones, and men use purple.

fukusabasami 帛紗挟み
Lit., "fukusa clasp." A clutch in which to keep one's fundamental personal chanoyu items.

furo 風炉
Brazier. Used to hold the live charcoal which heats the kettle at the temaeza. Conventionally they are used during the warmer part of the year (in Japan, around May to October), which therefore is called the furo season.

fushi 節
A node or joint. Bamboo tea scoops which are seen and used most often have a node positioned around the middle of their length.

fusuma 襖
A sliding door or wall panel made of thick paper covering a wooden inner framework, and encased on its four edges by a wooden frame.

futaoki 蓋置
Lid rest. Used to set the lid of the kettle on, and also to rest the cup end of the hishaku on.

geza (shimoza) 下座
The 'low seat'. This is the location countering the 'high seat' (*jōza*) in a traditional Japanese-style room where guests are received. Generally, the host's doorway is considered to be geza.

gotoku 五徳
Trivet. The iron three-legged stand upon which the kettle rests in the furo or ro.

gyō 行
This term literally means "going forth," and refers to the concept of "semi-formal." It is used in contrast to the terms *shin* and *sō*, which respectively refer to the concepts of "formal" and "informal." The formality hierarchy concepts of *shin*, *gyō*, and *sō* have relevance in almost all facets of chadō.

haiken 拝見
Respectful viewing. Term for the guests' studious viewing of the articles displayed in the alcove and at the temae-datami, and of implements used in the temae.

hanaire 花入
Flower container.

heri 縁
The bordering material on the lengthwise edges of tatami.

heri-soto, heri-uchi 縁外, 縁内
Heri-soto refers to the general area just on the other side of the lengthwise bordering of the tatami on which you are sitting; *heri-uchi* refers to the area just within that bordering.

higashi 干菓子
Lit., "dry confection(s)." The relatively small and dry confections conventionally served with usucha. As the guests may have several helpings of usucha, the host brings in a sufficient amount of higashi for the guests to be able to have a second serving.

hiki-bishaku 引き柄杓
Name for one of the three manners of setting the hishaku on the kettle during a furo temae. The other two are *oki-bishaku* and *kiri-bishaku*.

hiroma 広間
A tatami-floored room at least 4.5 tatami in floorspace.

hishaku 柄杓
Water ladle. The three types used for temae are made of bamboo. The water ladle used at the tsukubai (*tsukubai-bishaku*) is made of Japanese cedar.

jikyaku 次客
The guest who is second in order following the shōkyaku, or first guest, who is considered the main guest.

jōza (kamiza) 上座
The 'high seat'. The tokonoma is considered the highest place in a Japanese-style room, so the space in front of it is considered jōza. The main guest conventionally sits at or closest to this space. The contrasting 'low seat' location in the room is called geza (shimoza).

kaisaki 櫂先
The scoop portion of a chashaku.

kaishi 懐紙
A special kind of pocket paper. Kaishi come in packets which are folded in half from the beginning. The paper can be used for many purposes. A sheet of women's kaishi is about 175 mm x 145 mm. A sheet of men's kaishi is about 206 mm x 175 mm.

kakemono 掛物
Lit., "hanging." This refers to the scroll which is hung in the alcove or other such special display space. Also referred to as kakejiku.

kama 釜
Kettle. For chanoyu, cast iron handle-less kettles are used. There are many styles.

kamiza 上座
See "jōza"

kashi 菓子
Confection. This is the base term, but it is almost always used with the polite prefix, "o."

kashibachi 菓子鉢
A serving bowl for omogashi.

kashiki 菓子器
Lit., "confection container." This is a general term for any bowl, tray, or other container used to serve confections.

kashikiri 菓子切
A pick for cutting and eating omogashi. It may also be referred to by the more general term, *yōji*.

kattetsuki 勝手付き
This refers to the side of the temae tatami (temaedatami) that is closer to the mizuya and further from the guests. Normally, it is the left-hand side of that tatami. The side closer to the guests is referred to as *kyakutsuki*.

keiko 稽古
Practice; chadō practice session. The word is commonly used with the polite prefix, "o": okeiko.

keikoba 稽古場
The place where practice sessions regularly occur.

kensui 建水
Waste-water receptacle, into which water used to rinse the chawan is emptied.

kiri-bishaku 切り柄杓
Name for one of the three manners of setting the hishaku on the kettle during a furo temae. The other two are *oki-bishaku* and *hiki-bishaku*.

kiridome 切止
Cut end. The sliced-off end of hishaku and chashaku handles.

kiza 跪座
The "seated while kneeling" position. When getting down to sit seiza or getting up from sitting seiza, this is the

initial position taken. Your heels are together, the balls of the feet are on the floor with toes flexed forward, and your weight rests on your heels.

kobukusa 古帛紗
Specially sewn square of fine fabric used in the practice of chadō, mainly in connection with the handling and display of precious articles. A standard kobukusa is approximately 15 x 15.9 cm.

koicha 濃茶
Lit., "thick tea." Matcha of thick consistency, prepared by carefully blending the green-tea powder with the hot water. Usually enough to serve several guests is prepared in a single tea bowl. Koicha is the centerpiece at formal tea gatherings (chaji).

kojakin 小茶巾
Small wiping cloth. Guests who have drunk koicha each use a damp kojakin that they have brought with them (or which the host may provide) to wipe the part of the tea bowl's rim from which they drank. The kojakin is like a standard chakin, but is approx. 2/3 smaller.

kojakin-ire 小茶巾入れ
Case for the small wiping cloth (kojakin).

koma 小間
Lit., "small room." A tea room that is no more than 4.5 tatami in floorspace.

kuromoji 黒文字
A pick or pair of chopsticks carved from spicebush (kuromoji) wood, with the bark left intact on the side of it which is held in the hand.

kyaku 客
Guest(s).

makkyaku/tsume 末客／詰
Last guest. The guest who is in the last seat. The guest in this position should be able to handle certain duties which are helpful to the first guest and the host.

matcha 抹茶
Lit., "powdered tea." This can refer to the green-tea powder and also the usucha or koicha beverage made from it by blending it with hot water.

meimeizara 銘々皿
Individual plates.

mizuya 水屋
The preparation room connected to the tea room. The term mizuya, roughly meaning "water quarters," alludes to the fact that this is a space where water is available for rinsing, filling, and otherwise readying things.

natsume 棗
The most common variety of container for tea powder used in temae to make usucha (usuchaki). They are called natsume owing to their resemblance in shape to the jujube fruit (natsume). The great majority of natsume are lacquerware.

nijiriguchi 躙口
A type of small doorway for guests, as a rule seen exclusive in small tea rooms (koma). The door itself is wooden and slides open and closed. To enter through a nijiriguchi requires bending through from a crouching posture, then getting all the way through with legs folded beneath the thighs, as in seiza "correct sitting," and moving mainly using your arms to push you forward, backward, or around as needed. This manner of moving while in a seiza position is called nijiru, from whence the name of this doorway derives.

obi 帯
The kimono sash which is wound around the waist area.

ojigi お辞儀
Bow. The base term is jigi, which is almost always used with the polite prefix, "o."

okashi お菓子
See "kashi"

okeiko お稽古
See "keiko"

oki-bishaku 置き柄杓
Name for one of the three manners of setting the hishaku on the kettle during a furo temae. The other two are kiri-bishaku and hiki-bishaku.

omogashi 主菓子
Lit., "main confection(s)." The relatively large and moist confections conventionally served with koicha, one per guest.

ro 炉
Sunken hearth. The fire pit built into the floor of a chashitsu, used to heat the water in the kettle. It is used during the colder part of the year (in Japan, around November to April), which therefore is called the ro season.

roji 露地
The garden path leading from the waiting room to the tea room. The term "roji" literally means "dewy ground."

sadōguchi 茶道口
The host's doorway. Used by the host to enter/exit the tea room.

seiza 正座
Lit., "correct sitting." In Japan and in chadō, seiza is the formal, proper way to sit on the floor, with the legs folded beneath the thighs.

sekiiri 席入り
The tea-gathering guests' act of entering the room where the tea will be made and served (chaseki).

sensu 扇子
Folding fan. In chadō, a particular kind of folding fan is used. It is a representative item that guests keep on their person and use to express respect. Women's sensu are approx. 15 cm in length; men's are approx. 18 cm in length.

shikiita 敷板
A board, generally of wood which may be plain or lacquered, upon which something is placed. The size and type will depend upon its intended use.

shiki-kobukusa 敷古帛紗
The special small-sized kobukusa used in the Chitose-bon temae. The size is approx. 12 x 12.5 cm.

shimoza 下座
See "geza"

shin 真
This term literally means "true/correct," and refers to the concept of "formal." It is used in contrast to the terms *gyō* and *sō*, which respectively refer to the concepts of "semi-formal" and "informal." The formality hierarchy concepts of *shin*, *gyō*, and *sō* have relevance in almost all facets of chadō.

shōji 障子
A window, sliding wall panel, or partition made of a framed wooden (sometimes bamboo is used) grid covered on one side with paper which is thin enough to let the sunlight filter through.

shōkyaku 正客
First guest. This person generally is the most highly regarded/ranking among the guests at a particular seating. The first guest is generally expected to act as representative for all the guests.

sō 草
This term literally means "grassy," and refers to the concept of "informal." It is used in contrast to the terms *shin* and *gyō*, which respectively refer to the concepts of "formal" and "semi-formal." The formality hierarchy concepts of *shin*, *gyō*, and *sō* have relevance in almost all facets of chadō.

sōrei 総礼
All-together bow. The formal *shin* bow made simultaneously between the host and guests together.

teishu 亭主
Host. Conventionally, the person who conducts the temae. In a wider sense, the person who is presenting the hospitality.

temae 点前
Tea procedure. The prescribed method of preparing matcha in front of a guest or guests.

temaedatami 点前畳
The tatami in the tea room on which, in its upper half or upper portion, the equipment for the temae is arranged, and on which, in its lower half, the host sits and conducts the temae. Also called the *teishudatami* (host's tatami) or *dōgudatami* (tea-making equipment tatami).

temaeza 点前座
The place to sit in order to conduct temae.

tetsubin 鉄瓶
A lidded cast iron teapot. It has a pouring spout and a handle that crosses over the lid. Silver versions of this sort of teapot are called *ginbin*.

tokonoma/toko 床の間／床
Alcove. This is an architectural feature in traditional Japanese rooms. It is considered the 'highest' place in the room (jōza). Articles of great import, mainly calligraphic or pictorial scrolls, but also flowers and other items, are displayed here.

tsukubai 蹲踞
The low, stone water-basin arrangement along the garden path (roji) leading to the tea room, for rinsing hands and mouth and symbolically purifying body and mind before entering the tea room.

tsume 詰
See "makkyaku"

usucha 薄茶
Lit., "thin tea." Matcha of relatively thin consistency as opposed to the other form of matcha, called koicha or "thick tea." It is prepared in individual servings. In the case of a highly simplified tea service, it is the most common type of tea served.

usuchaki 薄茶器
The container for the green-tea powder used when conducting temae to make usucha. Natsume are the most common type of usuchaki.

warigeiko 割稽古
Lit., "divided practice." The beginning student's method of learning the fundamentals of temae by practicing each technique separately.

wasa わさ
The doubled-over edge of a fukusa, kobukusa, or other such double-layer item made of textile or paper. In the case of a fukusa or kobukusa, the other three edges are sewn together in an invisible fashion.

yōji 楊枝
Pick for eating confection.

yojōhan 四畳半
Lit., "four-tatami-and-a-half." Traditional style Japanese rooms of this floorspace, including tea rooms, are referred to by this term, *yojōhan*. Tea rooms having this number of tatami (4.5) are regarded to be of the key size for a tea room, the size which is neither strictly considered a small room (koma) nor a spacious room (hiroma).

Urasenke Tea Procedure Guidebook 1
Introductory Level

[英文] 裏千家茶道 点前教則 一
入門 割稽古・客の心得

2017年4月11日　初版発行
2025年7月18日　2版発行

著者　　一般財団法人 今日庵理事長　千 宗室
翻訳　　一般社団法人 茶道裏千家淡交会総本部国際部
　　　　（グレッチェン・ミトワ　マイケル・ハーディ）
写真　　宮野正喜　田畑みなお　小笠原敏孝
発行者　伊住公一朗
発行所　株式会社 淡交社
　　　　本社 〒603-8588 京都市北区堀川通鞍馬口上ル
　　　　営業 Tel.075-432-5156　編集 Tel.075-432-5161
　　　　支社 〒162-0061 東京都新宿区市谷柳町39-1
　　　　営業 Tel.03-5269-7941　編集 Tel.03-5269-1691
　　　　www.tankosha.co.jp
装訂　　株式会社 ザイン
印刷・製本　大日本印刷株式会社

©2017 一般財団法人 今日庵理事長　千 宗室
Printed in Japan　ISBN978-4-473-04178-4

定価はカバーに表示してあります。
落丁・乱丁本がございましたら、小社書籍営業部宛にお送りください。
送料小社負担にてお取り替えいたします。
本書のスキャン、デジタル化等の無断複写は、著作権法上での例外を除き禁じられています。
また、本書を代行業者等の第三者に依頼してスキャンやデジタル化することは、
いかなる場合も著作権法違反となります。